ZOMBIES!

ZOMBIES!

An Illustrated History of the Undead

Jovanka Vuckovic

with Jennifer Elss

Foreword by George A. Romero

ST. MARTIN'S GRIFFIN
NEW YORK

ZOMBIES! An Illustrated History of the Undead

Copyright © 2011 by Ilex Press Limited.
All rights reserved.

Foreword © 2011 George A. Romero

All images copyright © their respective
copyright holders.

For information, address St. Martin's Press,
175 Fifth Avenue, New York, N.Y. 10010.

www.stmartins.com

Library of Congress
Cataloging-in-Publication Data
Available Upon Request

ISBN-13: 978-0-312-65650-8

This book was conceived,
designed, and produced by
I L E X
210 High Street,
Lewes,
East Sussex,
BN7 2NS
www.ilex-press.com

For Ilex:
Publisher: Alastair Campbell
Creative Director: Peter Bridgewater
Managing Editor: Nick Jones
Editor: Ellie Wilson
Commissioning Editor: Tim Pilcher
Art Director: Julie Weir
Designer: Jon Allen

First U.S. Edition:
February 2011

10 9 8 7 6 5 4 3 2 1

Printed in Thailand

Color Origination by
Ivy Press Reprographics

Main title font set in Shlop
© Ray Larabie
www.larabiefonts.com

CONTENTS

Foreword

Okay, so here's the thing. For forty-three years, now, I have spent a great deal of time—too much time, I think—hanging out with dead people. I am not a necrophile. I have found some of the female-dead attractive (usually because their make-up artists, serving some producer's will, have been dedicated to making them look sexy). But while the dead, once fed, seem to be fairly submissive, I prefer the warmer embrace of a woman who still has a heartbeat. As to the males of the species, they (again, once they are fed) exhibit behaviors that put living males to shame. While they occasionally belch and fart (details I have chosen not to exploit in my films for fear of creating a negative bias) they never lie, they never get drunk, they rarely scratch their balls, and they never hog the TV, insisting on "sports" while I would rather watch a classic movie.

So, all things considered, I prefer the dead over the living.

I can't tell you how PISSED-OFF I get when I see a dead person treated rudely by any of the hundreds of filmmakers who are making "zombie films" these days. Did you ever see those commercials: "It's so easy, even a caveman can do it"? Then we see a caveman, wearing Gucci and sipping a vintage Cabernet, getting so irritated that he goes stalking off. I can only wonder what a dead person must think when it sees itself similarly insulted by a ridiculous movie that depicts the dead as mindless and insignificant.

And even if a zombie aspires to be another Jim Brown, it knows, in its heart . . . whatever is left of its heart . . . that it can't RUN! Its ankles would snap off! And that would greatly inhibit not only its movements but its ability to catch whatever prey is constantly running away from it.

In recent years, authors have tried to find "reasons" for the existence of zombies. There's some sort of virus. Or the government has exposed people to a dreadful carcinogen. Or cell phones are turning the masses into mindless masses. Such authors—and some of them are my friends—seem to be missing the point. The point is that if there ever is a so-called "zombie apocalypse," whatever super-power (dare I mention "God" or "The Devil") it was that created you and I, has changed the rules on us.

Death used to be a sort of a reward, the reward of sleep without any sort of an alarm clock. Churches have threatened us for centuries with a fiction that predicts that once we die we will be judged and subsequently be sent either to Heaven or to Hell. I say, "horse-puckie!" We ain't goin' NO-where, man! We are probably going to just . . . blink out. Nothing left.

But who wants to believe that? I mean, REALLY believe it? Not you, nor me, not The Good Humor Man.

Underneath everything, I believe I am here to stay. I believe that if I was removed, simply removed from the mix, that the world would be somehow worse for it. I want to think that I am important enough to be a permanent part of what we call "life." I think zombies and zombie fiction (because nobody can ever presume to be writing zombie FACT) in a strange way, gives us hope.

Jovanka "The Vook" Vuckovic has given us, here in the book you are holding in your hands, a history of the "zombie" in film and literature. Just remember, as you read this book, that . . .
. . . some day YOU are going to die.
And when you do . . .
. . . and when you come back . . .
. . . try to be a "good guy."

George A. Romero

Introduction

They are lifeless, gloomy, and sometimes smell worse than a meat-rendering plant after a month-long power outage. Some lumber about aimlessly with vacant stares while others sprint—blackened teeth gnashing—in hot pursuit of our brains. They are zombies. And despite their offensive odor and relentlessly poor fashion sense, they've managed to worm their way into the hearts of the living all over the world. From films to video games to musicals, comic books, and even global "zombie walks," the zombie has firmly established itself as the most beloved mythical monster in mainstream popular culture.

The most familiar image of the zombie is that of a recently unearthed, dentally challenged, slack-jawed cadaver shuffling about moaning in its burial garb, but a look back at the creature's history reveals that, like the living, no two zombies are equal. Myriad tales of bodily resurrection appear in the ancient myths, legends, and folklore of the people of the world's history. But there is one constant among these tales: they all feature beings that have somehow managed to physically return from oblivion to walk the earth. By this definition a vampire is also a zombie, albeit a highly specialized ghoul characterized by a distinctive thirst for blood. But for the sake of space and simplicity, we'll consider the fanged living dead (which, unlike the zombie, possess consciousness and free will) in their own category, and they will therefore not be included in this book.

It's difficult to pinpoint the exact origin of the zombie in mythology, because many folkloric tales are told through the oral tradition, which naturally tends to disappear over time if not retold. But as the Egyptians illustrated so well, there are alternatives to recording a culture's history on paper. As early as circa 2400 BC, Osiris was depicted on stone as a green-skinned god of the Underworld, a Lord of Death that returned from the afterlife to impregnate his lover Isis, who assembled his dismembered body parts and reanimated him (incidentally, legend has it she never recovered his penis and inventively fashioned one out of clay).

Other tales of early zombism emerged via resurrection texts in Babylonian and Northern Semitic mythology (such as Tammuz from Kur, a Summerian King who may have conquered death after a great flood), and, according to fundamentalist Christians, God raised an entire valley of dead bones (possibly belonging to the Ephraimites, one of the twelve tribes of Israel) to living flesh and blood before Ezekiel's eyes. Most notably, Jesus Christ also had the power to raise the dead and allegedly did so many times during his ministry. As the story goes, after his own death by Roman crucifixion, he was entombed and subsequently returned to bodily life in the flesh three days later. This alleged resurrection is considered by many devout Christians as an actual event and is the foundation of the Christian faith, making Jesus of Nazareth the most popular zombie in Western belief. While not everyone is a believer, this story has nevertheless been religiously passed down for over two thousand years and remains one of the most widespread tales of zombism in recorded history.

This raises the question: why are zombies so prevalent in world mythology? Perhaps it is because they symbolize and exemplify our temporary relationship with our bodies. Many

LEFT: **Don Siegel's *Invasion of the Body Snatchers* (1956) presents a very zombie-like apocalypse.**

ABOVE: **Impressivley leathery make-up in Nazi zombie movie *Shock Waves* (1977). Image courtesy Blue Underground.**

of us fear committal to the grave—a place from which we cannot return, despite the best efforts of voodoo practitioners, black magicians, and mad scientists. For a culture that typically views life and death as two distinct and irreversible states of being, the zombie represents the possibility of conquering death, though I'm not sure why anyone would want to return to life under the condition of ceaseless putrefaction. For the zombie, death is not the end. Rather, it is merely a minor inconvenience before returning victorious, having escaped the clutches of the grave. But the condition of un-death also begets universal philosophical queries about identity and the nature of what it is to be human. In this case, being undead is generally regarded as being worse than dead. In other words, we are less afraid of dying or being eaten by a zombie than we are of becoming one. Even worse: seeing our loved ones completely bereft of emotion and personality (which is the greatest strength of the *Invasion of the Body Snatchers* films). This is perhaps most relevant in the case of the Haitian zombie, which calls into

question the metaphysical state of un-death; being alive and dead at the same time.

Long before the word "zombie" entered the *Oxford English Dictionary* in 1819, it had been uttered in the voodoo rituals of Afro-Caribbean religion and folklore. Voodoo (or voudoun) beliefs are commonly maligned, misunderstood, and most often associated with the Haitian Republic—a place made famous by the West via books such as *The Serpent and the Rainbow* and films such as *White Zombie*. While not technically reanimated corpses (because they don't ever officially stop living but are merely transformed into something other), Haitian zombies are often people serving out punishment for cultural wrongdoing at the hands of voodoo practitioners by having the most valuable possession taken from them: their individuality. Here a zombie is defined by a separation of his or her own consciousness. The gruesome and tragic history of slavery in the region by French plantation owners, along with William Seabrook's exaggerated writings about the place in his

LEFT: **Key art for** *Let Sleeping Corpses Lie* **(1974) depicting zombies infecting the long-dead by placing blood drops in their eyes. Image courtesy Blue Underground.**

famous 1929 book, *The Magic Island*, led to the notorious wide-eyed, emotionless face of the voodoo-enslaved somnambulist of 1930s cinema.

The zombie has held a firm grip on the public imagination since it first appeared in literature and, despite its various handicaps, has consistently evolved (mostly on the silver screen) from mindless slave to flesh-hungry reanimated corpse (thanks to George Romero), to wisecracking, full-tilt running, virus-infected zombies capable of bringing about the apocalypse. Today, the myth of the zombie as a symbol of changing cultural anxieties (slavery, unemployment, brainwashing, disease) is stronger than ever, in part because the creature itself is quite adaptable and malleable. Every year it finds new unlife in various forms—be it as an adaptation of a literary classic, such as Seth Grahame-Smith's *Pride, Prejudice and Zombies*, or as an interactive video game in which players may assume the role of the infected and become zombies themselves, such as the *Left 4 Dead* series. The undead can be found in music, fine art, philosophy, and even children's cartoons.

Though *ZOMBIES!* is by no means definitive (such an undertaking is impossible in 176 pages), presented here is a selected overview of the evolution of the zombie from its early beginnings in African religion to its current status as one of the most culturally relevant mainstream horror figures—in all its gory glory. Bon Appetit!

Jovanka Vuckovic

CHAPTER 1

ORIGINS OF ZOMBIES IN HISTORY

Origins

Though the zombie had long been spoken about in hushed tones among American slaves in the late-eighteenth century, the mysterious monster didn't come to the attention of the American public until 1889, courtesy of author, traveloguist, and sensational journalist Patrick Lafcadio Hearn (1850–1904). Best known for his books about Japanese folklore, such as the story collections *In Ghostly Japan* (1899) and *Kwaidan* (1904), Hearn also visited the West Indies in 1887 and spent two years on location in Martinique penning a duo of books about the local culture called *Two Years in the French West Indies and Youma* and *The Story of a West-Indian Slave*, respectively. In the latter, Hearn claims that while in Martinique he "fell under the influence of that singular spell which the island has always exercised upon strangers."

ABOVE: **William Seabrook, under protection of machete and flag, in Haiti, ca. 1928.**

Fascinated by local tales of ghosts and zombies, he set about interviewing as many islanders as he could about something called "corps cadavers" or "walking dead"—a superstition he found particularly troubling given the nickname of the island: "Le pays des revenants," or, "The Country of the Comers-Back."

However, after much investigation, the locals only offered vague and conflicting anecdotes about three-legged animals and great fires, and Hearn was left to speculate about the creatures, which he mentioned in one of a series of articles he wrote for *Harpers Magazine* about Caribbean customs and folklore. His 1889 essay, "Country of the Comers-Back," became the first published study of zombies, pre-dating William Buehler Seabrook's famous *The Magic Island* by forty years.

Seabrook, an American Lost Generation journalist and adventurer, arrived in Haiti in 1928 with the express purpose of getting to the bottom of the zombie, or *le cults des mortes* ("the cult of death") mystery, which he would publish in a culturally denigrating autobiography festooned with illustrations of voodoo priests and priestesses engaged in "blood-maddened, sex-maddened, god-maddened" rites and rituals. The book, and the wild tales of black sorcery it told, was a sensation in America and went on to inspire a Broadway play followed by a film called *White Zombie* in 1932.

Seabrook was the first to actually describe three zombies he claimed to have encountered in broad daylight as "plodding like brutes, like *automatons,*" a description that would set the standard by which the creatures would appear in early American zombie cinema ... but we'll get to that later. A notorious sensationalist, hedonist, occultist (he was friends with Aleister Crowley), self-proclaimed cannibal, alcoholic, sadist, and

sexual thrill-seeker (who ended up committing suicide by overdosing on sedatives), Seabrook's account is indeed questionable but remains the first English text dedicated to understanding the phenomena of the Haitian zombie, however sensational and misrepresented they are.

Of the book's 336 pages, only twelve pages are devoted exclusively to the zombie in a chapter called "...Dead Men Working in the Cane Fields." In it, Seabrook describes his meeting with a farmer by the name of Constant Polynice, who regales him with tales of vampires, witches, werewolves, and other Haitian monsters, including the a local creature called the *zombi*. Familiar with all but one, Seabrook writes:

It seemed that while the zombie came from the grave, it was neither a ghost, nor yet a person who had been raised like Lazarus from the dead. The zombie, they say, is a soulless human corpse, still dead, but taken from the grave and endowed by sorcery with a mechanical semblance of life—it is a dead body which is made to walk and act and move as if it were alive. People who have the power to do this go to a fresh grave, dig up the body before it has had time to rot, galvanize it into movement, and then make of it a servant or slave, occasionally for the commission of some crime, more often simply as a drudge around the habitation or the farm, setting it dull heavy tasks, and beating it like a dumb beast if it slackens.

Polynice goes on to assure Seabrook that the zombie was no superstition, that even the poorest peasants, when they can, bury their dead beneath solid tombs of masonry in their own yards and near busy roads and footpaths "to assure the poor unhappy dead such protection as we can." He also indicates the islanders are very much aware of the zombies but do not interfere as long as their own dead are left

ABOVE: **Papa Nebo, flanked by Gouedé Mazacca the Midwife and Gouedé Oussou the Drunken One. These are sorceresses who use corpses for magical purposes.**

15

unmolested, then offers to show Seabrook dead men working in the cane fields of Hasco, an immense factory plant owned by Haitian-American Sugar Company—which had in the summer of 1918 offered a bonus on the wages of new workers on its own plantations.

As the story goes, one morning an old black headman by the name of Ti Joseph led a band of shuffling, dazed creatures to work at Hasco. The ghouls stared vacantly when they were asked to give their names. These were zombies dragged from their peaceful graves to slave for their master in the sun. They were kept in camps and fed bland food, for everyone knew the zombies were not permitted to taste salt . . . or meat. Ti's wife Croyance felt pity for the zombies and led them to see a local celebration at Croix de Bouqet. Here they were accidentally fed salty stew, which caused them to awaken from their spell and wander off into the mountains, where they were recognized by their family members. Once the zombies were restored to their graves, Joseph was cursed by a *bokor*, or voodoo priest, and subsequently beheaded for his crime.

Not entirely convinced, Seabrook does more "research" and ends the chapter by meeting with one Dr. Antoine Villiers, who indicates there may be criminal sorcery involved in the matter of zombies. As proof, Villiers produces a copy of the Criminal Code of the Republic of Haiti and points to a paragraph that reads as follows:

Article 249. Also shall be qualified as attempted murder the employment which may be made against any person of substances which, without causing actual death, produce a lethargic coma more or less prolonged. If, after the administering of such substances, the person has been buried, the act shall be considered murder no matter what result follows.

"No matter what result follows" . . . including the dead rising from their graves.

OPPOSITE: **"No one dared to stop them, for they were corpses walking in the sunlight." Alexander King's line drawing of Croyance leading the zombies, from the original edition of W. B. Seabrook's *The Magic Island*.**

ABOVE: **Alexander King's line drawing of . . . the dark mother of mysteries, from the original edition of W. B. Seabrook's *The Magic Island*.**

Dead Man Working:
A Brief History of Zombies in Haiti

The history of the zombie can be traced directly to the moment African slaves arrived in Haiti, a beautiful tropical paradise with a deeply troubled history. In 1492, Christopher Columbus discovered the island in the western Atlantic Ocean, which was then inhabited by the Taíno, an Arawakan people who called their island Ayiti, Bohio, or Kiskeya. The explorer reclaimed the island for Spain and renamed it Hispañola. Shortly after settling, the Spanish colonists had all but wiped out the indigenous population—possibly through exposure to Old World diseases, for which they had no immunity, and murder via enslavement. Sadly, the few Taíno who were able to escape into the mountains eventually became extinct after the last generation died out.

Céſt à ce prix que vous mangez du ſucre en Europe.

Candide Chapitre 19

ABOVE: **"It is at this price that you eat sugar in Europe." This 1787 engraving is from Voltaire's** *Candide.* **It depicts the scene where Candide and Cacambo meet a slave of a sugar mill who had his hand cut off for getting a finger stuck in a millstone and his leg forcibly amputated for trying to escape.**

By 1664, French buccaneers had arrived and began to take over the island, eventually renaming it Saint-Domingue and establishing massive tobacco, indigo, cotton, and cacao plantations on the fertile northern plain. Seeking to bolster the waning indigenous population, along with the sugar cane industry, the French began to import Africans as slaves. By the 1780s, Saint-Domingue had become one of the richest colonies in the eighteenth century French empire, producing close to half of all the sugar and more than sixty percent of the coffee consumed in Europe—all courtesy of an estimated 790,000 African slaves, who were often literally worked to death on plantations. The conditions of slavery were so brutal that by 1789 the African slave population, unable to grow without constant resupply, dwindled to a mere 32,000.

The slaves brought with them their own religion, which varied among the hundreds of different tribes imported from Guinea, Congo, and Dahomey. Of particular importance was the practice of "voudou" (or voodoo, voudoun, vodun, and vodou, meaning "spirit" or "divine creature"), which, despite the French's attempts to outlaw it, managed to flourish. A new, syncretic religion emerged among the slaves as a result. It was a complex fusion of African animism and Roman Catholic Christian liturgy and ritual that eventually became known to Westerners as "voodoo."

The principle belief of West African voodoo is that there exists a supreme god called "Bondye," as well as lesser spirits known as the "loa." After voodoo came in contact with Roman Catholicism in Haiti, worshippers were obliged to disguise

their deities, and Bondye became associated with the Judeo-Christian God, while each of the loa became associated with the Catholic saints. Because Bondye is considered the creator and unreachable by people, Haitian voodoo worshippers, or vodouisants, focus their worship on the various loa, which can be divided into twenty-one nations, or families, each governing different spheres of life including fertility, agriculture, and death.

Like Catholics, voodoo worshippers believe the body and soul are separate, which serves the ceremonial practice of possession by the gods. Each service begins with a litany of prayers and songs, both Catholic and African, sung around a principle altar. The loa are called upon by a Houngan (voodoo priest) or Mambo (voodoo priestess) and asked to take control of one of the worshippers. This is only possible once the individual's soul has departed via a trance-like state that is induced by music and dance.

In the voodoo faith each person has two souls, one of which is everything that makes the individual who they are (called the *gros-bon-ange*). The other is their essential essence, or life force (*ti-bon-ange*). When the *gros-bon-ange* departs the body, the god is permitted to enter, speak, and act through it. It is believed that the family of the possessed benefits from the possession during these ceremonies. When the spirit departs, the individual's *gros-bon-ange* may return to its vessel and reap the blessings of the loa.

Here's where the concept of the zombie fits in: if the person's soul is separated from the body by

ABOVE: **This reproduction of George Morland's** *Execrable Human Traffick, or The Affectionate Slaves* **(1789) depicts the sale of a slave, who is being separated from friends and relatives.**

19

CRUELTY OF THE WHITES TO CAPTURED RIOTERS.

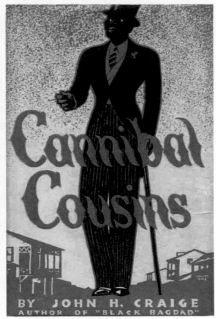

Cannibal Cousins

BY JOHN H. CRAIGE
AUTHOR OF "BLACK BAGDAD"

FAR LEFT: **"Santa Cruz: Scenes and Incidents of the Recent Insurrection and Incendiarism of the Negroes of the Island."** An illustration of a labor riot by Alfred Rondier, from *Frank Leslie's Illustrated Newspaper* (1878).

LEFT: **John Houston Craige's** *Cannibal Cousins* **(1934) details Haitian customs and practices in the early 1900s when he was with the U.S. Marines, and later as the Chief of Police in the nation's capital, Port-au-Prince.**

a *bokor*, or evil sorcerer, the victim's soul may never regain entry to its body, leaving behind an empty shell vulnerable to enslavement. A *bokor* is able to accomplish this using a combination of magic and potent potions capable of inducing a death-like state (see Haitian Voodoo Zombie Powder, p. 22). Once the person has "died" and their soul has been captured, the necromancer then retrieves the corpse from the grave and resurrects it as a mindless slave in his or her control. The revived, obedient slave is referred to as *zombi*.

It's not surprising belief in the zombie flourished in Haiti during that time, given the large number of seemingly mindless, and near lifeless, drones working on plantations. Robbed of their individuality and free will, the beaten-down African slave worker would have surely had the appearance of the living dead. The zombie was widely believed to be a very real creature in Haiti and thus affected funerary rites and burial passages; families would bury their dead under heavy masonry so the corpse could not rise from the grave. Those who could not afford headstones would bury their deceased relatives near roadways and watch over the gravesite until sufficient time allowed for

adequate decomposition. Otherwise it would be possible for a *bokor* to resurrect the body and use it for slave work elsewhere on the island where it would not be recognized.

Because a person's most valued possession—especially in a cruel slave nation—was their individuality, the Haitians' primary fear was not of being attacked or eaten by a zombie, but of becoming one themselves. It was considered a fate worse than death, the ultimate horror, particularly after the Haitian revolution, during which the nation finally overthrew its European oppressors. Not surprisingly, the slaves invoked voodoo to begin the revolution. In a famous voodoo ceremony conducted in August of 1791, a spirit possessed a Mambo—a voodoo priestess—who received a black pig as an offering, and all who were present vowed to fight for freedom. This ultimately led slaves in the northern region of the colony to stage a bloody revolt that began the Haitian revolution and culminated in the liberation of the Haitian people from French colonial rule in 1804.

Naturally, this didn't please Napoleon Bonaparte, who sent in 40,000 troops to reclaim the new

"Black Republic." French troops failed to regain control of the island, but the country was left in ruins. Revolutionaries struggled over the next century to maintain the country's development in the face of several regime collapses, social unrest, and bankruptcy. Many leaders were assassinated and the nation fell into chaos and debt. Then-President General Guillaume Sam, who was criticized by his political opponent Rosalvo Bobo for his dealings with the U.S., was assassinated and publicly dismembered by an unruly mob after he executed 167 political prisoners who threatened his power.

Guillaume Sam's dealings with the U.S. resulted in a $21 million dollar debt to American banks and eventually led to U.S. military occupation by 1915. Although the U.S. was present in Haiti under the pretence of re-establishing order and basic needs (education, plumbing, medical care, and construction of roads), it was really there to prevent a foreign nation such as Germany from recruiting the impoverished and unstable republic into war against the United States. Rather than helping, the American soldiers made a further mess of Haiti and tried to remake it in their own image by imposing segregation and forced unpaid labor on chain gangs (under penalty of death) as well as introducing the word "nigger" to the Haitian vocabulary.

This brings us back to William Seabrook's *The Magic Island*, which was published at the height of America's occupation and control of Haiti and was a huge success. It capitalized on American beliefs that Haiti was a nation of savage cannibals by sensationalizing voodoo and offering a vague explanation for the existence of the zombie—one that hinted at evil, possibly Satanic, ritual as the culprit. Other books of dubious authenticity such as John Houston Craige's *Black Bagdad* [sic]: *The Arabian Nights Adventures of a Marine Captain in Haiti* (1933) and *Cannibal Cousins* (1934) followed, featuring exaggerated tales of wild rituals, evil potions, and bodily resurrection.

Before anyone knew it, the zombie had officially reached American consciousness.

ABOVE: **The cover of John Houston Craige's** *Black Bagdad: The Arabian Nights Adventures of a Marine Captain in Haiti* **(1933), his allegedly true story of crash landing in Haiti and being forced to watch his fellow marine get killed and eaten.**

Haitian Voodoo Zombie Powder

If there's one person who can be called an authority on the existence of real life zombies, it is anthropologist, ethnobotanist, and author Wade Davis. In 1982—after studying plants in the Amazon basin and the Andes for three years—Davis traveled to Haiti to discover the voodoo folk preparation that was allegedly being used to turn people into zombies. What he found there consumed his life for four years.

Like everyone else who'd grown up exposed to sensationalistic books such as *Cannibal Cousins, Black Bagdad, Voodoo Fire in Haiti, A Puritan in Voodooland, The Magic Island,* and *The White King of Lagonave* (written typically by white military Southerners hailing from a world of segregation in America during the twenties), Davis had heard about the zombies of Haiti, but dismissed their existence as exploitive nonsense. "There were dozens of these books," Davis recalled in a 2009 interview. "And they were all filled with children bred for the cauldron, pins and needles in voodoo dolls that do not exist, and zombies crawling out of the grave to attack people."

According to Davis, a zombie—by Haitian folk definition—is a "living dead," an individual who has been magically brought to his end,

LEFT: **From 1982 to 1986, noted anthropologist Wade Davis studied the pharmacological components of Haitian voodoo "zombie powder" and discovered its most consistent ingredient—a neurotoxin extracted from Fugu "puffer" fish—had the ability to make its victims appear clinically dead.**

ABOVE: **A Haitian bokor grinding a folk preparation implicated in the alleged creation of zombies. Photo copyright Wade Davis.**

only to be somehow magically resuscitated, to be led away to a life of enslavement. Davis didn't believe in this folkloric idea of magic, but his interest was piqued when he uncovered a curious set of reports in ethnographic literature and in the accounts of missionaries and other popular writings on Haiti citing cases of legitimate zombism. One that stood out was a case psychopharmacologist Nathan Kline had documented, which concerned a folk poison that was said to bring on a state of apparent death so profound it could fool a physician.

In the early 1980s, a Haitian student of Kline's named Lamarque Douyon, along with a colleague of his, Heinz Lehman, were interested in a possible connection between pharmacology and the zombie. Though they too did not believe in magic, it was not inconceivable that a drug could exist that would bring on a state of apparent death so convincing that it could fool a western-trained physician.

"What really shifted this from the realm of the phantasmagoric into the realm of the possible was the discovery of this curious case of a man called Clairvius Narcisse by Douyon in 1980 or '81," Davis recalled. "Narcisse had died at the American Philanthropic Institution, the Schweitzer Hospital. Because of that, there were impeccable

medical records that gave a clear account of the death of this individual, which was witnessed by his family members. His medical condition at the time of his demise is properly recorded and so on. This death occurred in 1963." None of this was unusual, except for the fact that a man claiming to be Narcisse turned up in the same village in 1980. Scotland Yard fingerprints and family interviews confirmed that this man was none other than the long-deceased Narcisse.

"In Haiti, a zombie is a complete pariah, so no one would boast or make up the notion that they'd been a zombie any more than a leper in Hyde Park Corner in London would stand up and boast of his disease," explained Davis. "So all these lines of evidence led Douyon, Kline, and Lehman to go public on the BBC in 1981, saying they felt they had found the first medically verifiable instance of a zombie."

Through interviews with various *bokors*, negative priests, and sorcerers, Davis was able to secure several different chemical preparations of "zombie powder," all of which turned out to

have consistent ingredients—everything from snakes and toads to various plants and human remains—for magical purposes. But the critical and interesting ingredient was one of a number of species of a genus of puffer fish called the Fugu, a very well-known tropical fish that is also the source of the famous Japanese delicacy.

According to biomedical literature from Japan, the Fugu fish has within it the most powerful neurotoxin ever discovered from nature: Tetrodotoxin (also known as "tetrodox" and frequently abbreviated as TTX), which is about one hundred times more poisonous than potassium cyanide as a drug and has no known antidote. A lethal dose of the pure toxin would balance on the head of a pin. "But more interestingly is the way that it kills," Davis elaborated. "It's this big molecule that selectively blocks sodium channels in the nerves, which brings on peripheral paralysis, dramatically low metabolic rates, and yet amazingly, consciousness is retained until the moment of death. Now, in Japanese literature, there was case after case after case

ABOVE: **The highly fictionalized and sensationalistic film adaptation of Wade Davis' bestselling book was released in 1988 from director Wes Craven.**

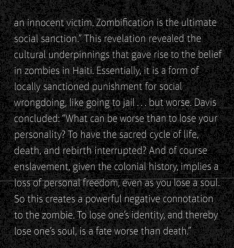

of people nailed in their coffins by mistake. Being laid out by your grave for three days is a folk custom in parts of Japan—to make sure you're really dead."

According to Davis, TTX was precisely the consistent ingredient in the Haitian folk preparations called "zombie powder." That discovery instantly moved the whole zombie phenomenon from the realm of the phantasmagoric into the realm of the possible, demonstrating beyond a shadow of a doubt that in a situation completely removed from Asia, the Haitian sorcerers had identified in their environment a natural product that had a drug in it that could make people appear to be dead. From then on, Davis' hypothesis became rooted in the underlying concept of "Tetrodotoxin Zombification."

"Any drug that creates an ambivalent potential for good or evil creates a template upon which belief systems can go to work," explained Davis. "In Haiti, a zombie is not an innocent victim. It's a person who has transgressed the rules of the society and is being sanctioned. Narcisse wasn't

an innocent victim. Zombification is the ultimate social sanction." This revelation revealed the cultural underpinnings that gave rise to the belief in zombies in Haiti. Essentially, it is a form of locally sanctioned punishment for social wrongdoing, like going to jail . . . but worse. Davis concluded: "What can be worse than to lose your personality? To have the sacred cycle of life, death, and rebirth interrupted? And of course enslavement, given the colonial history, implies a loss of personal freedom, even as you lose a soul. So this creates a powerful negative connotation to the zombie. To lose one's identity, and thereby lose one's soul, is a fate worse than death."

Davis' research could not be substantiated (due to lack of clinical trials on humans) and there has since been much speculation from the scientific community regarding the effects of TTX.

Nevertheless, the anthropologist recorded his experiences in a 1983 paper, followed by a 1985 book, *The Serpent and the Rainbow*, which became the basis for the highly fictionalized, eponymous horror film from director Wes Craven.

ABOVE LEFT: *Serpent and the Rainbow: A Harvard Scientist's Astonishing Journey into the Secret Societies of Haitian Voodoo, Zombis, and Magic:* Wade Davis' account of real-life zombies in Haiti.

ABOVE RIGHT: **"Zombie powder" is rumoured to contain dead human tissue along with the drug Tetrodotoxin. It is collected here in a human cranial cap.**

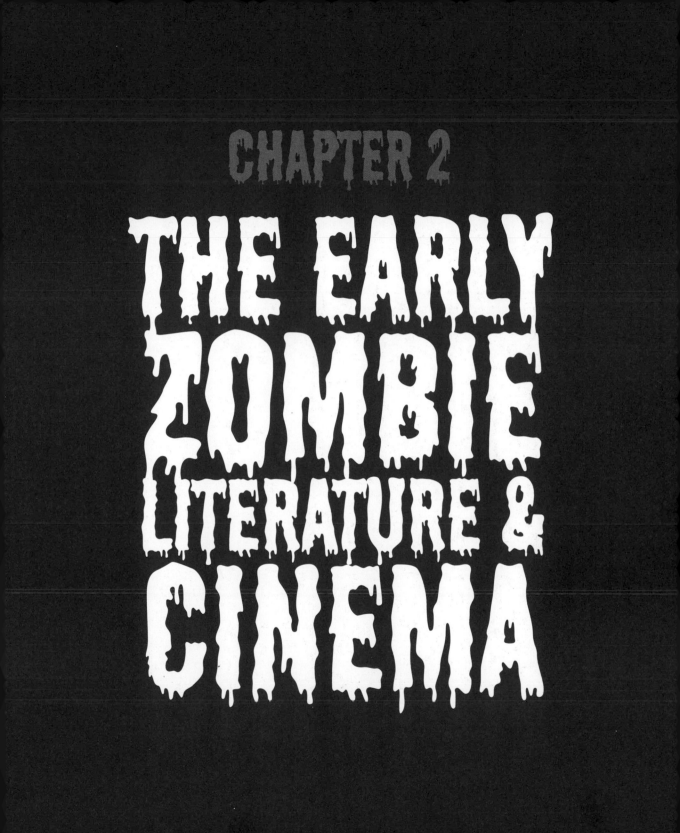

CHAPTER 2

THE EARLY ZOMBIE LITERATURE & CINEMA

Early Literature

Unlike the vampire, the zombie's literary roots cannot be traced to a specific point of origin (*à la* John Polidori's 1819 short story *The Vampyre*). Instead, the zombie popped up in various incarnations as early as 1706, when the English language edition of *One Thousand and One Nights* (or *Arabian Nights*, as it is most commonly known) appeared in print. The collection of Middle Eastern and South Asian stories and folktales includes a proto-zombie lit story entitled "The History of Gherib and His Brother Agib" (from *Nights*, vol. 6) about an outcast prince (Gherib) who vanquishes an army of undead ghouls and converts them to Islam.

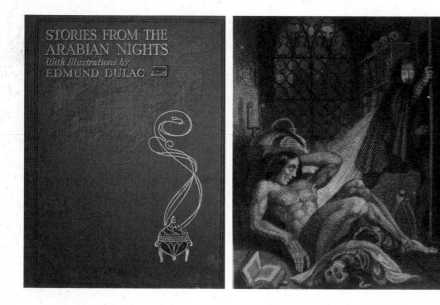

FAR LEFT: **Zombies in literature can be traced back as far as 1706's *One Thousand and One Nights*. Reprinted here is the cover of the book *Stories from the Arabian Nights* (1907) by Laurence Housman.**

LEFT: **Detail from frontispiece of Mary Shelley's *Frankenstein*.**

Perhaps the most famous published story about a walking, talking undead is Mary Shelley's *Frankenstein; or, The Modern Prometheus*. In contrast to later film adaptations, Shelley's monster was not comprised of reassembled human remains. In fact, it is never revealed where Victor Frankenstein procured the body for his monster, but it is hinted that the creature is similar to a golem—an anthropomorphic being created from lifeless clay. Although not a zombie story proper, Shelley's 1818 novel prefigured the mad scientist story, as well as the twentieth-century concept of the resurrection of the dead as a scientific process resulting in creatures that

are resentful of their creators and more violent than their human counterparts. The novel deftly explores existential themes of loneliness, the relationship between creator and creation, and the universal desire for acceptance. Like the original Greek Prometheus of the book's subtitle, Dr. Frankenstein is ultimately punished for playing god.

It wasn't long before the gothic tale finally featured vengeful reanimated corpses, though. "The Death of Halpin Frayser" by Ambrose Bierce (1893) is a prominent example, in which a woman named Catherine Larue rises from

DEEP, DEEP, AND FOREVER, INTO SOME ORDINARY
AND NAMELESS *GRAVE*

" I WOULD CALL ALOUD UPON HER NAME "

the dead to kill Halpin Frayser. She is described in the story as a "lich," which is a special type of ghoul that can recognize its friends and relatives (whereas a zombie is typically only capable of distinguishing the living from the dead). It is a proto-zombie tale that expands on the notion of the undead being more violent or "evil" than they were while alive. The woman turns out to be Frayser's own mother, which opened the story up to later Freudian interpretation.

Although never having written explicitly about zombies per se, Edgar Allan Poe was known for having an obsession with death. His tales are replete with people being buried alive before rising as vengeful ghouls. Case in point: "The Premature Burial" (1844) and its narrator, who is beleaguered by random death-like trances of catalepsy. Understandably, the man bears a crippling fear of being buried alive; should he lapse into one of his spells and be mistaken for dead, he may be interred too soon (much like the zombies of Haiti, which were people who were drugged into a death-like state and reanimated as slaves). But Poe's preoccupation with what lies beyond the grave didn't end with "The Premature Burial." Another story, "Ligeia"

CLOCKWISE FROM TOP LEFT:
An illustration by Harry Clarke depicting Edgar Allan Poe's "The Premature Burial." From a 1928 publication of *Poe's Tales of Mystery and Imagination.*

"Ligeia," by Harry Clarke, from a 1928 publication of *Poe's Tales of Mystery and Imagination.* Ligeia is a woman who refuses to die after her body does.

Illustration for Edgar Allan Poe's gory proto-zombie tale, "The Facts in the Case of M. Valdemar" by Harry Clarke (1889–1931). Published in 1919.

FAR LEFT: **It Came from the Pulps!** After appearing in questionable travelogues in the early twenties, the Haitian zombie cut its teeth in pulp magazines such as this extremely rare issue of *Weird Tales* (September 1926), which included the first publication of Henry S. Whitehead's "Jumbee." Cover by E. M. Stevenson.

LEFT: *Weird Tales* (March 1940) featuring Manly Wade Wellman's "Song of the Slaves." Cover by Hennes Bok. © coll. Maison d'Ailleurs/Agence Martienne.

(1838), tells of a woman who refuses to die when her body does, and "The Fall of the House of Usher" (1839) revolves around Roderick Usher's growing anxiety over having buried his sister alive. Usher is convinced he can hear her scratching at her coffin lid, trying to escape. She eventually returns from the grave emaciated to seek vengeance on her brother. Poe brought the zombie one step closer to unlife in "The Facts in the Case of M. Valdemar" (1845), about a man (the narrator) who hypnotizes a tuberculosis-afflicted author (Valdemar) at the precise moment of death to see if he can gain control of his victim. Valdemar physically dies but remains "alive." Though his skin is cold and dead and he lacks a pulse, Valdemar remains in a hypnagogic state for seven months, until the narrator attempts to awaken him. Speaking through a blackened, swollen tongue, Valdemar begs for death before his body quickly decomposes into a "nearly liquid mass of loathsome—of detestable putrescence." Unlike the rules of Haitian folklore, which permit authority over death through black magic, Poe's gruesome ending indicates that any attempt to appropriate power over death will be hideous and unsuccessful.

Poe's work (as well as the fiction of Lord Dunsany) had a profound influence on American fiction writer H. P. Lovecraft, by his own admission. But it was Mary Shelley he was deliberately channeling when he penned a grisly homage of bodily resurrection by (weird) science entitled "Herbert West—Reanimator" (1921). In the tale, Dr. West attempts to revive several corpses, all of which return as extremely violent, uncontrollable monsters. Unlike Frankenstein's monster, West's victims are actually plucked from fresh graves and are not thrilled about the disturbance of their slumber. Lovecraft later penned other undead-themed short stories such as "In the Vault" (1925; in which a character is actually bitten by a zombie), "Pickman's Model" (1927), "Cool Air" (1928), "The Thing on the Doorstep" (1937), and the superlative "The Outsider" (1926; in which the narrator actually is a zombie). Although all of them deal in the undead and other things that should not be, none of the creatures in Lovecraft's tales were referred to as "zombies." That word didn't catch on until the late 1920s, with the release of William Seabrook's Haitian travelogue, *The Magic Island*.

Due to the popularity of those early travelogues, in the mid- to late-1920s the Haitian zombie began to emerge in the short stories of the pulp magazines, alongside Lovecraft's short tales. The first was Henry S. Whitehead's "Jumbee" (*Weird Tales*, September 1926), about a man who happens upon a corpse-like spirit that hovers in the air. Whitehead served as Archdeacon to the Virgin Islands in the West Indies from 1882 to 1932 and allegedly based this story loosely on his real-life encounters with zombies in St. Croix. "Jumbee" was followed by Garnett Weston's "Salt Is Not for Slaves" (*Ghost Stories* magazine, August 1931), which warned readers about the dangers of feeding zombies salt, an action that awoke them from their sleep and returned them to their graves. On the strength of the short, Weston (who wrote the story under the pseudonym G. W. Hutter) was selected to write the screenplay for the movie *White Zombie* (1932), by director Victor Hugo Halperin. The same year, August Derleth contributed "The House in the Magnolias" (*Strange Tales* magazine, June 1932). Derleth, who would later go on to found the legendary horror publishing company Arkham House, set his story in New Orleans in an effort to bring the zombie closer to home. The zombies are created via African voodoo, taken into bondage, and imported to the United States by dark-skinned outsiders to work on plantations.

"Song of the Slaves" by Manly Wade Wellman (*Weird Tales* magazine, March 1940), about an unscrupulous white plantation owner who imports and subsequently murders forty-nine African slaves, is also concerned with how slavery is transplanted to the United States. But its distinguishing feature is the fact that its forty-nine murdered slaves return from the grave with vengeance—not mindless slavery—on their agenda. Even this early on, the zombie was beginning to evolve.

As popular as the pulps were, it wasn't until the zombie appeared in cinema that it became firmly established in the public consciousness and began its real evolution as a mythological creature. Zombie fiction, as it were, wouldn't pick up again until many years later.

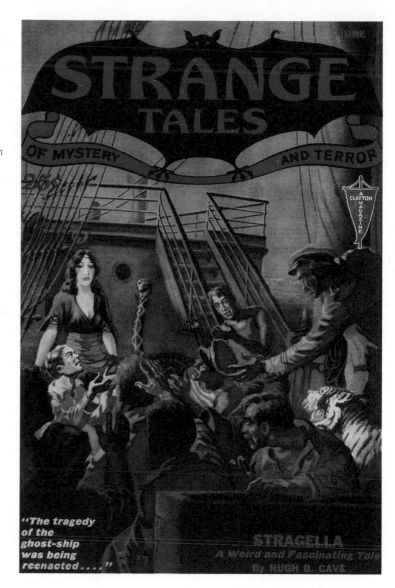

ABOVE: **"The House in the Magnolias," August Derleth's early tale of zombie slave revolt on a Southern U.S. plantation appeared for the very first time in this issue of *Strange Tales* magazine, June 1932.**

The 1930s

By the time William Seabrook's *The Magic Island* reached American readers, the horror film had already begun its initial rise to mainstream popularity. Early German expressionist silent features such as *The Student of Prague* (1913), *The Cabinet of Dr. Caligari* (1919; itself a zombie story without the element of death), *The Golem* (1920), and *Nosferatu* (1922) paved the way for American movie producers to cash in on the prominence of the new genre, which was made even more popular by a series of horror-themed stage productions including *The Bat* (1920), *The Monster* (1920), *The Cat and the Canary* (1922), and the hugely successful adaptation of Bram Stoker's *Dracula* (1927) from director Horace Liveright.

Soon the public would flock to the cinemas in droves to see the first horror movie star—the great Lon Chaney Sr.—transform himself into a hideous monster in *The Hunchback of Notre Dame* (1923), *The Monster* (1925), *The Unholy Three* (1925), *The Phantom of the Opera* (1925), *London After Midnight* (1927), and other early silent horror films.

Universal Pictures, then considered a second-rate studio to MGM, achieved enormous success with its line of horror films, among them Tod Browning's *Dracula*, starring Bela Lugosi (the first horror "talkie"), and James Whale's *Frankenstein*, featuring Boris Karloff. Both titles set the standard for American horror in 1931 and opened the floodgates for monster movies from every major studio, with Universal leading the way.

The following year, a stage production inspired directly by Seabrook's tales of Haitian voodoo and zombism opened to a lukewarm reception. Written and produced by playwright Kenneth S.

Webb and simply titled *Zombie*, the Broadway play failed to elicit any genuine scares, received mediocre to poor reviews, and closed after just twenty days. But the production remains significant because it served as the inspiration for *White Zombie*, America's first zombie film, produced and directed by brothers Edward and Victor Halperin.

Unlike the uninspired play it was based on, *White Zombie* (1932) had a lot going for it despite its meager $50,000 budget. It was written by Garnett Weston, who was handpicked by Halperin on the strength of his short story "Salt Is Not for Slaves," and shot by Arthur Martinelli, who had dozens of film credits to his name. It was also one of the first few independent productions (not funded by one of the big studios) to secure mainstream distribution and even featured a big name star: an overacting, post-*Dracula* Bela Lugosi, reportedly working for a mere $800.

TOP: **Robert Wiene's early expressionist film *The Cabinet of Dr. Caligari* (1919) is arguably a proto-zombie film in that it features a mindless somnambulist under the control of an evil hypnotist.**

ABOVE: **Werner Krauss as Dr. Caligari and Conrad Veidt as his enslaved sleepwalker, Cesare.**

OPPOSITE: **Madge Bellamy (Madeleine Short Parker) is zombified using a voodoo potion by wealthy plantation owner Murder Legendre (Bela Lugosi), but Charles Beaumont (Robert Frazer) is not happy with the result, in *White Zombie* (1932), the first bona fide zombie movie.**

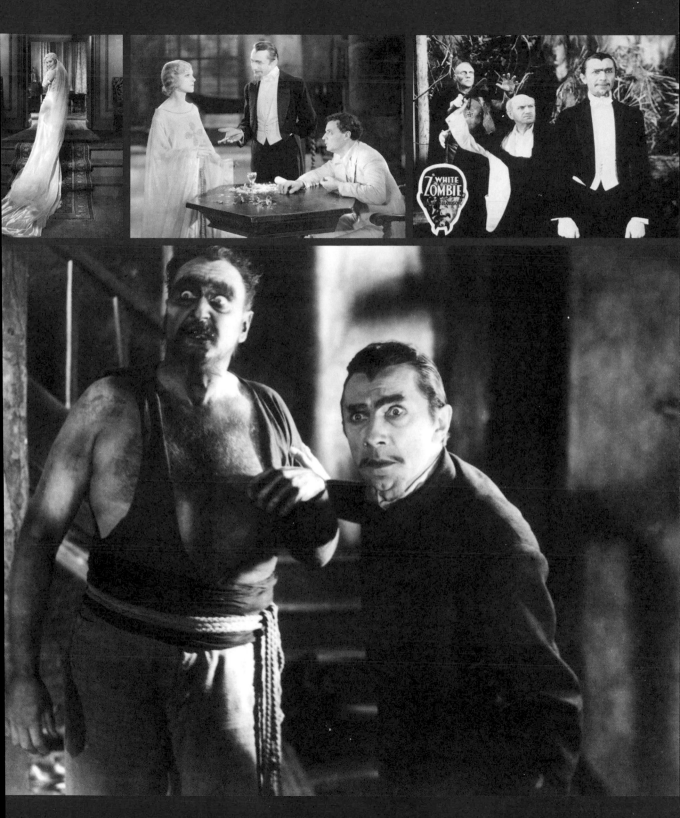

ABOVE:
Film poster for *White Zombie* (1932), directed by brothers Edward and Victor Halperin.

Lugosi had just turned down the role of the Monster in Universal's *Frankenstein* due mostly to vanity and hubris (famously claiming, "I'm an actor, not a scarecrow!" after a make-up test). The role went instead to newcomer Boris Karloff, whose portrayal of the monster went on to become one of the most recognizable movie monsters in cinema history.

By the time the Halperins approached Lugosi to appear in *White Zombie*, *Frankenstein* was an unparalleled success and the actor had learned his lesson. Now desperate for work, he jumped at the chance to play "Murder" Legendre, a wealthy European plantation owner who has discovered the secrets of voodoo. Murder uses drugs to zombify the locals and transform them into mindless brawn to slave on his sugar mill in Haiti. He is soon hired by a wealthy American named Charles Beaumont (Robert Frazer) to help him steal the affections of a beautiful woman named Madeleine Short Parker (Madge Bellamy), who is visiting with her fiancé Neil Parker (John Harron). Murder obliges by offering Charles a potion he procured from a voodoo priest, which he then doses Madeleine with

on her wedding night. The potion gives the woman the appearance of being dead but, of course, she is only in trance and is later claimed from the grave and revived by her zombie master at his estate. Unbeknownst to Charles, Murder has plans to keep Madeline for himself (why would anyone ever trust a guy named "Murder" to hand over a pretty lady anyway?). When she is united with her new suitor, Charles is unhappy with her new zombified state and begs to have the spell reversed. Murder responds by dosing Charles, who is then forced to watch the villain take his would-be bride into

servitude (for what remains unclear, but it's fair to assume his motivations are sexual). All is not lost, though, because amidst the sinister goings-on, Madeline's bumbling fiancé Neil manages to arrive at Murder's castle (which looks painfully like the redressed set of *Dracula*, because it is); vanquish the villain, Charles, and his hordes (who all fall to their deaths off a cliff); and revive his bride with the help of a missionary doctor played by Joseph Cawthorn.

Apart from a somewhat creepy opening scene and some inspired camerawork, *White Zombie*

CLOCKWISE FROM TOP LEFT:
The original illustrated film poster for *The Mummy* (1932).

Boris Karloff as The Mummy.
© Universal Pictures

A 1932 lobby card featuring Boris Karloff as the titular creature in *The Mummy*, a film that disassociates the zombie from its Haitian origins.

ABOVE LEFT TO RIGHT:
Boris Karloff is wrongfully executed and brought back to life by a scientist in 1936's *The Walking Dead*.

Behind the scenes of *The Walking Dead*: Boris Karloff with make-up artist Perc Westmore. © Warner Bros.

didn't turn out to be the fright fest the Halperins had hoped it would be. Critics panned the supporting cast's wooden acting and Lugosi's beyond-overcooked performance. Screenwriter Weston did the story a favor by taking a page right out of *The Magic Island*—setting the film on a Haitian sugar cane plant and featuring ritualistic burials and voodoo rites—but the redressed *Dracula* set looked far too much like a gothic castle to evoke the setting of an exotic plantation. The zombies themselves, being mindless slave workers who literally plummet off the cliff like lemmings, aren't much of a threat and therefore aren't very scary. Still, the necrophilic subtext ("A zombie bride performing every wish of he who had her by his magic"), a ghoulish new monster, the sensational "based on true events" publicity campaign, and pro-American topical subtext put asses in seats.

It is widely agreed that the Haitian zombie's timely arrival in the U.S. was the perfect reflection of cultural anxieties in Depression-era America. With entire families in financial ruin, nearly everyone faced the grim reality of joining the defeated drones in the breadlines—robbed of their dignity and personal autonomy. And although the film never acknowledges the American occupation of Haiti outright (doing so would destroy the illusion the filmmakers were trying to put forward), it certainly makes no bones about painting Haiti as a savage nation in need of American military intervention, thereby silently supporting the country's presence on the island. America, after all, was only there to stop a European nation such as Germany from appropriating the island into its military forces. This is symbolized in the struggle between Murder (an evil European) and Neil, a Christian American hero who saves the day. Without his intervention, Murder may have taken control over the entire island. Instead, he and the doctor aim to civilize the island and erase the presence of the Europeans.

Though mauled by critics, *White Zombie* managed to rake in over eight million dollars at the box office. But despite the film's success, the zombie as a movie monster remained persona non grata for the most part and was relegated to appearing in a series of low-budget horror flicks, including George Terwilliger's obscure film *Ouanga* (1936), about a jealous black female plantation owner who exacts revenge on her white male neighbor for choosing a white woman over her. It also toyed with American anxieties surrounding the Depression and occupation of Haiti. But moviegoers quickly became bored with the concept—especially after America ended its occupation of the Caribbean. In response, film producers made quick work of severing the tie between Haiti and the zombie. By this time, Lugosi's rival Boris Karloff had already appeared in three zombie-themed films that completely dropped the association with Haiti: the hugely successful *The Mummy* (1932), the haunted house production *The Ghoul* (1933), and *The Walking Dead* (1936), a stylish fusion of the gangster drama and horror film genres that remains a minor classic.

When the Halperins released *Revolt of the Zombies* (1936), the unofficial sequel to *White Zombie*, audiences had already lost interest in the racial anxieties of the Haitian zombie, so the new writers (Howard Higgin and Rollo Lloyd) decided to set the story in the Far East. Though Lugosi was not involved with the sequel, that didn't stop the filmmakers from ludicrously superimposing recycled footage of Lugosi's mesmerizing eyes over the scant few voodoo sequences. *Revolt* is set in Cambodia during the First World War and recycles much of the romantic plot from *White Zombie* with the addition of a Cambodian zombie army. The film had the potential to be interesting if it had bothered to tackle the concept of the soldiers' loss of personal identity. Instead, it focuses too much on an insipid love triangle between an officer in the French army (Dean Jagger) and his wife (Dorothy Stone), who is obsessed with his best friend. (Note: Abel Gance's 1938 zombie soldier film *J'accuse* is a far more sophisticated

commentary on the effects of war on people serving in the military.) The result was a tedious, poorly acted, agonizingly paced outing worthy of the critical lashing it received. *Revolt* did, however, possess one distinguishing feature: it was the first time the zombie was presented as a massive horde, prefiguring the apocalyptic zombie movies to come.

Other films of the period further divorced the zombie from its voodoo heritage by injecting the mad scientist pretense into the story. *The*

ABOVE: **Boris Karloff is a zombie in 1933's *The Ghoul*.**

Scotland Yard Mystery (1934), later released in the U.S. as *The Living Dead* (1936), revolves around a doctor who has discovered a drug that puts people into a death-like trance in order to collect on their insurance policies. Boris Karloff took yet another turn as a zombie in *The Man They Could Not Hang* (1939). This time he played a scientist hanged for the attempted murder of one of his students, who offers himself up as the first human recipient of an artificial heart. Of course, the doctor doesn't stay dead long and he returns to punish everyone involved in his untimely death. *The Man They Could Not Hang* is less a zombie movie than the first in a series of scientist-gone-mad films.

And while the odd film such as 1939's *The Devil's Daughter* (a remake of *Ouanga*) echoed the trappings of voodoo, by the end of the 1930s it was extremely rare for such an association to be seen in zombie cinema. The lore of the zombie had been ripped wide open and was about to take a turn for the humorous.

ABOVE: **Although Boris Karloff (pictured) returns from the noose in 1939's *The Man They Could Not Hang*, it more closely resembles a mad scientist film. © Columbia Pictures Corporation**

ABOVE: An entire army of Cambodian zombie soldiers gets revenge in Victor Halperin's *Revolt of the Zombies* (1936), the hapless, unofficial sequel to *White Zombie*.

RIGHT: *The Scotland Yard Mystery* (1934; later released as *The Living Dead*) fully divorces the zombie from its Haitian origins as evinced by its tagline ("Not a ghost! Not A Vampire! NOT A ZOMBIE! What is 'The Living Dead'?").

The 1940s

The forties was a particularly lean decade for the zombie. The big horror boom of the thirties was over, America's men were at war, box office sales were down, and the big studios had for the most part lost interest in horror. Hollywood's "Poverty Row" studios began to pick up the slack but with diminished returns. And if that wasn't bad enough, the zombie was about to become the laughing stock of movie monsters. Before Paramount Pictures gave up on the zombie for the rest of the decade, it released what can be considered to be the first zombie-comedy with 1940's *The Ghost Breakers*, starring none other than Bob Hope.

Directed by George Marshall and shot to capitalize on the success of the previous year's mystery-comedy *The Cat and the Canary*, *The Ghost Breakers* recasts both comedian Bob Hope (as radio personality Lawrence "Larry" Lawrence) and Paulette Goddard (as Mary Carter) as an unlikely pair that travels to Mary's newly inherited castle estate off the coast of Cuba. The only problem is, the island is notoriously haunted by ghosts and inhabited by very real zombies. The castle itself is even guarded by a local undead woman named Mother Zombie (Virginia Brissac) and her undead son The Zombie (played to spooky perfection by Noble Johnson). In what is almost a *Scooby-Doo* set up, a gaggle of locals intend on scaring Mary off the island and keeping the secret silver mine underneath it. The ne'er-do-wells get up to some cheap spooky antics that are eventually solved by Larry and his black manservant Alex (Willie Best), who hilariously compete for the title of the film's biggest scaredy cat.

ABOVE LEFT: **Bob Hope in** *The Ghost Breakers* **(1940), with Paulette Goddard and Paul Lukas.** © Paramount Pictures

ABOVE: **The theatrical poster for the hugely successful horror comedy,** *The Ghost Breakers* **(1940).**

The Ghost Breakers' blend of humor and horror may have pleased audiences in the early forties, but there is no concealing its overt racial politics. It's no coincidence the story takes place on "Black Island," or that the two main (mindless) zombies are black, as well as Lawrence's bumbling manservant. Alex's demeaning jokes are uncomfortable by today's standards, as are Lawrence's references to "spooks." The highlight of the film for horror fans is, by far, Noble Johnson's portrayal of the son zombie. Unlike the pale-faced ghosts of zombies past, the creature is depicted as a disfigured ghoul that might actually be long dead—due to the application of a full facial prosthetic. The Ghost Breakers marks the first time such an appliance was used to portray a zombie. Despite the film's success, Paramount promptly abandoned the zombie from its film roster.

Poverty Row studio Monogram was more than happy to pick up the scraps and turned over a series of cheapjack terror tales beginning with the especially racist King of the Zombies (1941). Recycling the white investigator/black manservant theme from The Ghost Breakers, the plot sees pilot James McCarthy (Dick Purcell), along with Bill Summers (John Archer) and his black valet (Mantan Moreland), crash land on a Caribbean island during the Second World War while searching for a missing admiral. The island is inhabited by a Nazi-sympathizing scientist named Doctor Miklos Sangre, played by Henry Victor (the strongman from Tod Browing's Freaks) in a role originally intended for Bela Lugosi, who wisely passed on the script. Directed by Jean Yarbrough, King of the Zombies centers around Sangre's efforts to use voodoo to transfer the captured admiral's soul into another body to gain his military secrets. The film's concern with American race relations is patently obvious after Jeff the black manservant is zombified and "put back in his place," and skulks around acting like an idiot, which is where most of the comedy lay for whites in King of the Zombies. The rest of Sangre's zombies are lazy, witless drones that hang around the kitchen waiting for food— hardly a frightening image, but quite obviously a commentary on the derogatory view white America had of African-Americans at the time.

ABOVE LEFT TO RIGHT:
King of the Zombies (1941): A cheapjack terror tale from Monogram Studios modeled after *The Ghost Breakers* that wears its racial politics on its sleeve.

Bowery at Midnight (1942): Bela Lugosi is a gangster in this bloodless Monogram cheapie.

Revenge of the Zombies (1943): A dull horror comedy starring John Carradine as a Nazi scientist bent on creating an army of goose-stepping zombies to fight for Germany.

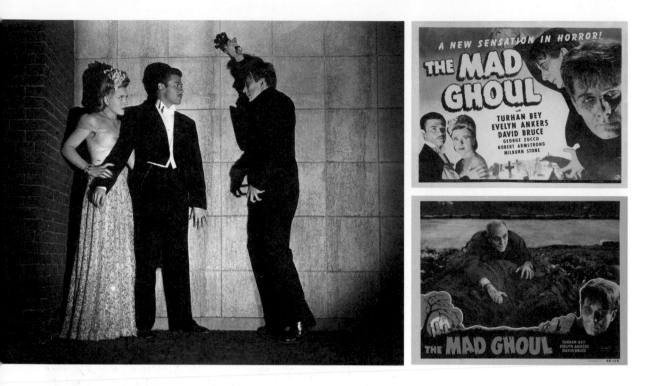

The film was a surprising success by Monogram's standards, so the studio wasted no time drumming up the painfully dull horror comedy sequel *Revenge of the Zombies* (1943), which recycled most of the plot from *King* and starred John Carradine as a Nazi scientist bent on creating an army of goose-stepping zombies to fight for Germany. In this case, the zombie is a product of science rather than voodoo. The creatures, by the doctor's supposition, could survive without food and sustain major bodily damage as long as the brain stays intact. This could possibly be the first time the zombie is cited as needing a brain to go on unliving, prefiguring George Romero's "must destroy the brain" pretence by nearly thirty years. But the movie's merits end there. As horror comedy, the film's biggest joke is the doctor's wife, who continues to refuse orders even after she is zombified. Oh and there's a hilarious black zombie named Lazarus, whose wild coiffure makes him resemble a young Don King.

Bowery at Midnight (1942) was the first of two Monogram cheapies that featured a legitimate star: Bela Lugosi, this time playing Professor

Frederick Brenner, criminal, husband, and owner of a New York soup kitchen. Ultimately it's a cops-and-robbers movie spliced with a zombie film (à la Karloff's *The Walking Dead*) that's weak on pretty much all accounts. The not-so-good professor uses his business as a front for a bevy of illegal activities perpetrated by a gang of thugs who work out of his basement. Brenner's been leaving the corpses of his accomplices at each crime scene, but unbeknownst to the boss, his basement dwelling mad-doctor-turned-drug-addled-conspirator (Lew Kelly) has been reviving the dead, who eventually get revenge on Brenner in the film's closing scene. Unfortunately the zombies only appear in a scant two scenes. Less a zombie movie and more a crime film, *Bowery* is one of the better Monogram cheapies of the day.

Good thing Universal decided to step up to the plate and release its first zombie film, a decent outing called *The Mad Ghoul* (1943). It's a Frankenstein-inspired tale starring Universal horror stalwart George Zucco as mad scientist Dr. Morris, who murders his assistant and controls his cadaver with an ancient Mayan nerve gas.

CLOCKWISE FROM ABOVE:
Universal releases its first zombie film with *The Mad Ghoul* (1943).

A lobby card from *The Mad Ghoul*, Universal's overlooked zombie melodrama.

George Zucco, Evelyn Ankers, and David Bruce in 1943's *The Mad Ghoul*. © Universal

Doc Morris' newly created zombie relies on human hearts to survive, which ends up serving the film's most chilling scenes of grave robbing. *The Mad Ghoul* remains one of Universal's overlooked classics.

The following year, Monogram was at it again, following up *Bowery* with an even more low-rent, creatively bankrupt zombie outing featuring Lugosi: 1944's *Voodoo Man*. Lugosi stars as another mad doctor who's been abducting women and attempting to transfer their souls into his zombie wife. The ridiculous film, which served to objectify women more than offer any legitimate scares, practically destroyed the careers of his co-stars, John Carradine and George Zucco, and signaled the beginning of the end of Monogram's zombie pictures.

On the opposite end of the quality spectrum stands 1943's haunting and lyrical *I Walked with a Zombie*, an RKO picture helmed by *Cat People* director Jacques Tourneur. Val Lewton was the head of RKO's horror division at the time, despite the fact that he personally hated horror films. Nevertheless, in an attempt to simultaneously turn profits for the ailing studio and create a truly suspenseful high-brow horror film, he hired Tourneur to direct what he intended to be a redux of *Jane Eyre* in the West Indies, with an exploitation title that appealed to horror fans. The result is a beautifully shot, remarkably understated, darkly poetic, slowly paced melodrama about a Canadian nurse (Betsy, played by Frances Dee) who travels to Antigua to care for Jessica, the catatonic wife of a wealthy plantation owner named Paul Holland (Tom Conway). The locals believe Jessica to be a zombie, and it is revealed that the wife had an affair with Paul's alcoholic half-brother Wesley. Nurse Betsy falls for Paul and becomes trapped in the middle of a love triangle between the brothers, who both vie for her affections. Oddly still desperate to help Jessica after conventional medicine has failed her, Betsy leads the invalid through the dark sugar canes to the island's hounfort—a voodoo temple—which is run by the mother of Paul and Wesley, as she's been

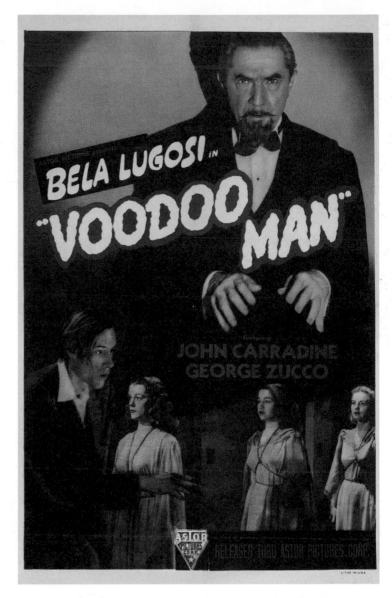

dabbling in voodoo. Along the way she meets and survives an encounter with Carrefour, a hulking local zombie (played by Darby Jones), who follows her but never really attacks her. It's a complex story that ends with Wesley drowning Jessica before killing himself, leaving the audience with more questions than answers.

The film's title was taken from an *American Weekly* article called "I Walked with a Zombie" by Inez Wallace. It was a questionable first-person account

ABOVE: *Voodoo Man* (1944): **Not even Bela Lugosi could save this low-rent follow-up to** *Bowery at Midnight.*

that blatantly plagiarized Seabrook's travelogue *The Magic Island*. But Lewton borrowed more from the article than just its title. Like the story, he returned the zombie to its Haitian roots but surprisingly handled voodoo with respect and took the opportunity to explore the deliberately unanswerable question of the true existence of zombies in the Caribbean. By far the best entry in the 1940s' zombie canon, *I Walked with a Zombie* is low on horror, high on romance, but evenly drenched with atmosphere, intelligence, and class.

Why then, after such a successful turn at the zombie film, RKO would want to follow it up with a thoroughly unwatchable comedy sequel remains one of the great mysteries of the cosmos. *Zombies on Broadway* (1945) had virtually nothing to do with the Lewton/Tourneur collaboration that preceded it besides the fact that it poached two actors from that film, notably Darby Jones in an embarrassing redo of his role in *I Walked with a Zombie*. Bela Lugosi is back again as a mad doctor, along with a second rate Abbott and Costello duo: the staggeringly unfunny Wally Brown and Alan Carney, who play press agents in charge of publicizing a new bar (!) called The Zombie Hut. They head out to a nonexistent island in the Caribbean to procure a zombie formula from Lugosi. Upon their return to the United States, much un-funniness ensues. Let's put it this way: when a comic monkey can out-act its human co-stars, you know you're in trouble.

The last zombie movie of the decade was another stinker, 1946's *Valley of the Zombies*. The film is incorrectly named as there is nary a zombie in sight, nor a valley for that matter. It's about an undertaker (Ian Keith) who, after taking part in some vague voodoo ritual four years ago, now requires constant blood transfusions to stave off the unpleasant side effects of his affliction. Eventually he takes to killing people and stealing their blood, but this misguided and weak thriller ends up being more of a lukewarm action-detective movie about a modern vampire than a zombie film.

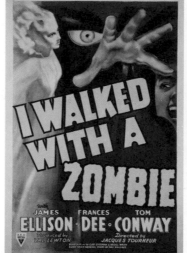
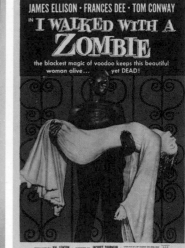

ABOVE, CLOCKWISE FROM TOP:
Two posters for the RKO production *I Walked with a Zombie* (1943).

Darby Jones as Carrefour, the passive local zombie in Jacques Tourneur's lyrical *I Walked with a Zombie* (1943).

OPPOSITE, CLOCKWISE FROM TOP:
The mad doctor (Bela Lugosi) and victim (Anne Jeffreys) in the horribly unfunny comedy *Zombies on Broadway* (1945).

Three lobby cards from *Zombies on Broadway* (1945), RKO's thoroughly unwatchable comedy sequel to *I Walked with a Zombie*.

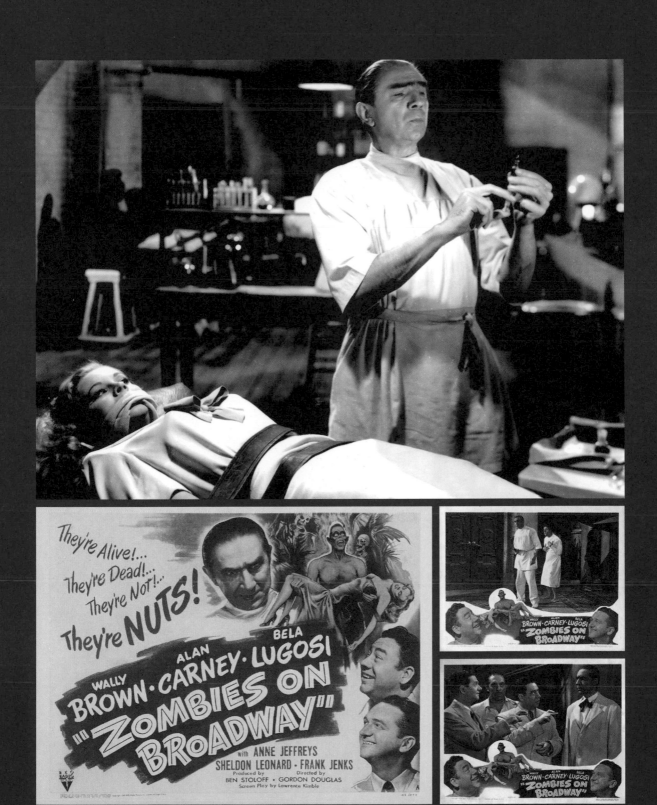

The 1950s

The 1950s is generally considered the worst decade for the zombie. The atomic bomb had been dropped, the Second World War was over, the automotive industry was booming, drive-ins were thriving, teenagers had replaced adults at the movies, the Cold War was setting in between America and the Soviet Union, and both nations had set their sights on the cosmos. Anti-Communism, nuclear anxiety, and fear of alien invasion were at an all-time high, and independent movie producers responded by producing and selling cheap, teenage-driven films that merged horror with science fiction to drive-in owners. Along with giant ants, bug-eyed aliens, and robots gone berserk, the zombie managed to rear its now-radioactive head throughout the decade in a series of (largely forgettable) films that generally replace the racial concerns of earlier films with more topical anxieties such as loss of personal autonomy and brainwashing.

First up was the falsely advertised *Zombies of the Stratosphere* (1952). Leonard Nimoy stars as one of three evil Martians that conspire to deflect Earth out of its orbital place using H-bombs in order to move their own planet closer to the sun. There are no zombies whatsoever, nor does any of the action take place in the stratosphere, making this stock footage-laden clunker (also released under the equally confusing title *Satan's Satellites*) definitely worth missing.

Seeking to capitalize on the success of *The Ghost Breakers* (1940), Paramount released a redux called *Scared Stiff* (1953) that replaced the comedy duo of Bob Hope and Willie Best with the much-less-funny Dean Martin and Jerry Lewis. It's pretty much the same movie but with an all-white cast, fewer laughs, more annoying dance numbers, and a blonde zombie (Jack Lambert) who makes a funny clicking sound when he walks. While a moderate success, it was quite clear that drive-in audiences of the 1950s were no longer interested in dusty old voodoo-themed zombie movies.

If things couldn't get more preposterous for the zombie, Edward L. Cahn managed to "atomize"

it in *Creature with the Atom Brain* (1955). Along with the help of an ex-Nazi scientist, exiled mobster Frank Buchanan (Michael Granger) revives corpses from the morgue using neural implants and a radioactive blood transfusion. They remotely control the zombies from their lab via a bar of radium and some simple voice commands spoken into a microphone. The resulting army of white, business suit-wearing undead goons are sent out to generally wreak havoc as they take revenge on the people who testified against the mobster. It's pure nuclear schlock that plays on fears of Communist mind control and pays homage to the zombie movies of the 1940s by having one of the zombies turn on its master in the end.

In a spasm of genius for the decade, Don Siegel's masterpiece *Invasion of the Body Snatchers* (1956) presents a dead serious zombie-like apocalypse of global proportions. In the film, humans are slowly replaced with emotionless alien impostors while they sleep. The pod people may look a hell of a lot like us, but they are strangers intent on establishing a new order—one devoid of personal autonomy. The film has been regarded as an allegory for loss of individuality in the Soviet

Union and even an underhanded criticism of McCarthyism. But *Body Snatchers*' most significant contribution to the evolution of the zombie is the fact that it deals with infection/invasion on a global scale. Not since 1936's *Revolt of the Zombies* has the idea of the zombie been associated with doomsday. In the film's finale, the two remaining survivors are pursued by a massive horde of zombie-like impostors. They may not be reanimated corpses, but the pod people stand in quite well for the living dead here.

The body snatching continued across the pond in Hammer Studios' *Quatermass 2* (1957). Also known as *Enemy from Space*, *Quatermass 2* centers on sentient vapors that hitch a ride to earth on meteors and begin possessing humans. Brian Donlevy reprises his role as the eponymous Professor Quatermass, a downtrodden scientist who investigates strange goings-on at a government facility he believes to be under alien control. Communist paranoia of the 1950s fueled much of the threat in zombie films of the era and *Quatermass 2* is no exception. Once again, the zombies are not the voodoo-enslaved other, but rather ourselves made other. Quatermass

ABOVE LEFT TO RIGHT:
Creature with the Atom Brain (1955): Zombies get jacked up with electronic circuits and radioactive blood in this nuclear shlockfest.

Humans are replaced by emotionless alien impostors in 1956's *Invasion of the Body Snatchers*.

The remaining two survivors are pursued by a zombie-like horde in Don Don Siegel's *Invasion of the Body Snatchers*.

Brian Donlevy reprises his role as the eponymous Professor Quatermass in *Quatermass 2*.

An Italian poster for *Quatermass 2* (1957).

A poster featuring the alternate title for *Quatermass 2*, highlighting the decade's obsession with extraterrestrial mind control.

OPPOSITE: **Dean Martin and Jerry Lewis make "spook-tacles" of themselves in this uninspired remake of *The Ghost Breakers*.** © Paramount Pictures

audiences of the 1950s. Voodoo dolls, carnivorous plants, and even outrageously fake underwater zombies (in *Zombies of Mora Tau*) couldn't save these films from dying derivative deaths at the box office. Similarly, Universal's soporific *The Thing that Couldn't Die* (1958) was too concerned with evil, Satanism, and the supernatural to entice audiences more interested in alien invaders.

This might explain why director Edward L. Cahn returned to the theme of totally implausible alien mind control in his third ultra-low-budget zombie film, *Invisible Invaders* (1959). The ludicrous plot sees aliens possessing the corpses of humans (mostly men in suits and ties) in an attempt to—what else?—conquer earth. Unfortunately the plot is as absurd as its zombies are rigid and unfrightening. Evidently the invaders were content to leave us alone as long as we stayed primitive, but our new nuclear powers have made us a threat to the galaxy and we must be destroyed. Scientists armed with high-frequency sound waves save the day but not before we're treated to the apocalyptic image of an army of alien-controlled foot soldiers rising up all over the planet. With their ashen faces, wooden gait, and sheer numbers, the zombies of *Invisible Invaders* no doubt provided inspiration for George Romero's iconic film *Night of the Living Dead* (1968).

LEFT TO RIGHT:
Zombies of Mora Tau (1957): The first (albeit fake-looking) underwater zombie film.

Voodoo Island (1957): An unsuccessful attempt to take the zombie back to its voodoo roots, starring Boris Karloff.

Not even a talking Satanic severed head could save *The Thing that Couldn't Die* (1958) from dying a derivative box office death.

eventually uncovers a conspiracy involving alien infiltration of the British government and saves humanity from becoming a race of mindless slaves under the control of malevolent aliens.

In 1957, three zombie films that unsuccessfully attempted to step backwards and return the zombie to its voodoo origins were released. *Voodoo Island* (starring Boris Karloff), *Womaneater*, and Edward L. Cahn's *Zombies of Mora Tau* are confused titles that failed to capture the attention of atomic-obsessed

Ed Wood took the grave robbers from outer space shtick to new lows in *Plan 9 from Outer Space* (1959), a risible zombie movie that bears the distinction of being labeled "The Worst Movie Ever Made." Two extraterrestrials named Eros and Tanna invade Earth on flying hubcaps and attempt to stop humanity from creating a doomsday weapon. For the task, they implement "Plan 9" and begin recruiting an army of zombies—three of them, to be exact—from the graves of the deceased. Tor Johnson, Vampira (Maila Nurmi), and a chiropractor pretending to be Bela Lugosi by covering his face with a cape spend the majority of the film skulking around the fakest looking cemetery set ever built as the most absurd and incoherent plot unravels around them. While *Plan 9* displays a depth of ineptitude, it has nevertheless earned a place in the hearts of bad movie lovers across the globe and remains one of the weirdest zombie movies ever made. See the movie then see the movie about the movie (Tim Burton's *Ed Wood*).

The last production of the decade to deal with the living dead might actually be worse than *Plan 9*. *Teenage Zombies* (1959) is a strictly homemade affair from Jerry Warren about a group of *Archie*-styled teens—named Reg, Skip, Julie, and Pam—who decide to go waterskiing but end up on an island inhabited by a female mad scientist who's working on a zombie gas for foreign powers. The kids are expectedly imprisoned by the femme fatale, but by the time a zombified gorilla (yes, a guy in an ape suit) discovers the antidote and saves the day, you'll be too stupefied to care. If you scrape at the bottom of the barrel until it falls through, you'll find *Teenage Zombies* there.

CLOCKWISE FROM ABOVE LEFT:
Zombies of Mora Tau director Edward L. Cahn was wise to return to the theme of alien invasion with his third and most influential zombie film, Invisible Invaders (1959).

Grave robbers from outer space revive corpses from cemeteries in Ed Wood's notorious zombie film, Plan 9 from Outer Space (1959).

Tor Johnson and Vampira (Maila Nurmi) play the alien-enslaved undead in Plan 9 from Outer Space.

The 1960s

Though the fifties was by far the leanest decade for the zombie, it was about to experience a resurrection in the psychedelic sixties. Up to this point, most movie zombies were little more than pale-faced ghouls, but the rot was about to set in. Thanks in part to the efforts of Mexican films such as Rafael Portillo's *The Aztec Mummy* series (starting in 1957)—which experimented with using rotting corpses as zombies—visibly composing cadavers began to appear more and more in the movies. As the putrefaction progressed, the zombie got scarier and not just because of its unsightly appearance. It was evolving along with the times, which were definitely a-changin'.

Beginning with films such as *Invasion of the Body Snatchers* (1956) and Alfred Hitchcock's *Psycho* (1960), the horror film shifted the focus from the terror without to the terror within. People were no longer watching the skies, but rather, their neighbors, loved ones, and even themselves. In these films, the zombies weren't bug-eyed aliens or voodoo-enslaved foreigners, they were ourselves . . . and they were virtually indistinguishable from us. Suddenly the established boundaries between "us" and "them" came crashing down, ushering in a new era of genre films that looked inward. But when it came to zombie films, America took its time sloughing off the established paradigms of the fifties in releasing alien-led tripe such as *The Cape Canaveral Monsters* (1960) and dull voodoo retreads such as *The Dead One* (1961)—one of the first two color zombie films.

The rest of the decade turned out to be a decidedly mixed bag for the United States: Boris Karloff paid his respects to the old-fashioned zombie with "The Incredible Doktor Markesan"

on his television show *Thriller* (1962), Roger Corman and Vincent Price brought Poe's "The Case of M. Valdemar" to life in *Tales of Terror* (1962), and cheapjack director Del Tenney made a mockery of *I Walked with a Zombie* with his gore-less and goofy *I Eat Your Skin* (1964). Tenney tried again with the truly terrible but surprisingly bloody *The Horror of Party Beach* (1964), which staggeringly insists on labeling mutated fish people with googly eyes as "zombies." A truly wretched beach dance number called the "Zombie Stomp" serves as evidence the filmmakers had no idea what a zombie is.

Things just got weirder when *The Incredibly Strange Creatures Who Stopped Living and Became Mixed-Up Zombies!!?* (1964; a.k.a. *The Teenage Psycho Meets Bloody Mary*) was released, billing itself as "the first monster film/musical." This mental mélange of bad lounge acts, humor, and horror really has nothing to do with zombies save for four hypnotized mutants that interrupt a musical

TOP: **The 1960s got off to a dull start with *The Dead One* (1961) a.k.a. *Blood of the Zombie*, one of the first color zombie films. America looked back to the established voodoo themes, while zombies the world over began to evolve.**

ABOVE: **A crazy mélange of bad lounge acts, humor, and horror that has nothing to do with zombies.**

number during the climax of the film. It was followed by a Z-rate anthology called *Dr. Terror's Gallery of Horrors* (1967) that included a segment in which a bloated, bleary-eyed Lon Chaney Jr. in the nadir of his career attempts to revive a cadaver. Then there was Ted V. Mikels' colossally clumsy and kitschy *The Astro Zombies* (1968), about a mad scientist who creates a machete-wielding, skull-masked "astro man" from a cadaver. Not even horror staple John Carradine and the busty cult icon Tura Satana could save this one from becoming a laughing stock of absurdity—a distinction that paradoxically earned it cult status among bad movie lovers. By the end of the decade, it was clear that Hollywood had lost interest in the walking dead, and they seemed destined to remain fodder for low-budget films helmed by seemingly low-talent directors.

Down in Mexico, zombies were shambling to an even sillier beat. Professional wrestling (where it's known as *lucha libre*) was one of the most popular forms of entertainment and its biggest star, El Santo (The Saint), began appearing in a series of wacky wrestling films that saw him facing off against a variety of supernatural enemies. A masked crusader who wrestled by day and fought crime by night, El Santo (real name Rodolfo Guzmán Huerta) was Mexico's answer to *Batman*, if only the caped crusader wrestled three full matches per episode. Santo

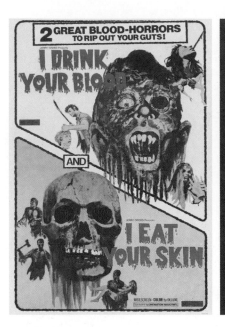

would go on to appear in roughly sixty features and vanquish all manner of conceivable adversaries from werewolves to evil brains to zombies. *Santo contra los zombies* was among his earliest exploits and it was released in the U.S. as *Santo vs. the Zombies* in 1962. When an evil scientist resurrects a bunch of dead thugs to commit crimes, Santo runs afoul of the doctor and his minions using his mad wrestling skills. Totally goofy and anything but scary, *Santo vs. the Zombies* would be the first of many times the Mexican icon would get in the ring with the recently resurrected.

Other Mexican productions followed, including the campy *Dr. Satan Versus Black Magic* (1968; a.k.a. *Dr. Satán y la magia negra*) and *Isle of the Snake People* (1968; a.k.a. *La muerte viviente*), starring Boris Karloff. Given the poor quality of these later Mexican titles, the Santo films sadly remain the best of the bunch.

Meanwhile, over in Spain, notorious sexploitation filmmaker Jess Franco took the subject just a little more seriously with his first zombie movie *Dr. Orloff's Monster* (1964). Conceived as a pseudo-sequel to the arty *The Awful Dr. Orloff*, *Monster* is little more than a pretentious, thinly veiled

exploitation flick about a zombie that stalks hookers and strippers. But the zombie didn't stop its travels there. It even found its way down to South America when Argentina weighed in with *The Deadly Organ* (1967; a.k.a. *Placer sangriento*), about a masked stalker who injects beach babes with heroin and uses organ music to transform them into his zombie slaves.

As the zombie languished in bargain basement obscurity all over the globe, the UK succeeded at properly resurrecting it. An early color zombie film from Canadian director Sidney J. Furie, *Dr. Blood's Coffin* (1961), is a strictly low budget affair from the UK that attempted to cash in on the popularity of Hammer Studios' gothic horrors—minus the "gothic." Kieron Moore stars as Dr. Blood, a Frankenstein-like doctor who conducts heart transplant experiments on cadavers in an attempt revive the dead husband of his love interest, Linda (played by Hammer scream queen Hazel Court). While abandoned Cornish tin mines make for a lush backdrop, *Dr. Blood's Coffin* is painfully slow and ultra-light on zombie action. In fact, there's only one flaky-skinned green zombie (the husband), and he doesn't appear until the last four minutes of the final reel, when he attacks his widow and strangles

ABOVE LEFT TO RIGHT:
Cheapjack director Del Tenney made a mockery of *I Walked with a Zombie* with his gore-less and goofy *I Eat Your Skin* (1964), released only as a double bill with the exploitation flick *I Drink Your Blood*.

***The Horror of Party Beach* (1964), "The First Horror Monster Musical," insists on labeling mutated fish monsters with googly eyes as zombies.**

Dr. Blood. Still, it's relevant for offering up a visibly decayed and extremely violent corpse rather than a pale-faced, aimless somnambulist—a hint at the more nasty things to come.

Hammer director Terence Fisher weighed in on the zombie craze with *The Earth Dies Screaming* (1965), a somewhat ridiculous apocalyptic horror/sci-fi about interstellar robots with giant glass domes for heads who use a poison gas to exterminate all life on earth, save for a few people who managed to hole up in airtight chambers or procure gas masks. Like 1959's *Invisible Invaders*, the aliens resurrect some extremely slow-moving cadavers to hunt down and eliminate the survivors. Because of budgetary restraints, Fisher was relegated to shooting in a handful of locations, which reduces the scale of the story but effectively centers the attention on a small group of survivors and their interpersonal dynamics. It's teeming with cheap-looking robots and clunky dialogue, but the fact that it places a handful of average citizens in the middle of a zombie apocalypse makes it an obvious precursor to *Night of the Living Dead*.

The same year saw the release of *Dr. Terror's House of Horrors* (1965), Amicus' British horror anthology from director Freddie Francis. It is notable for perhaps being the first movie to feature a zombie hand terrorizing a human being (Christopher Lee), while 1966's Nazi-themed *The Frozen Dead* makes hilarious use of entire limbs as well as a head. But by far the most influential British film of the decade is John Gilling's *The Plague of the Zombies* (1966). Unlike Hammer's first zombie film, *Quatermass 2*, *Plague* drops the science fiction element in favor of straight-up horror. The film pays homage to *White Zombie* (1932) by taking the traditional voodoo paradigm and transplanting it onto a Cornish village in England but amps up the gore and decomposing zombies.

The year is 1860. A mysterious epidemic is killing off workers in the village of Cornwall. Desperate and at a loss for a diagnosis, the local young Dr. Peter Tompson (Brook Williams)

ABOVE AND RIGHT: **A mad scientist creates a machete wielding, skull-masked "astro man" from a cadaver in Ted V. Mikels' colossally clumsy and kitschy *The Astro Zombies* (1968).**

enlists the help of his old medical school professor Sir James Frobes (André Morell) and his daughter Sylvia (Diane Clare). Upon their arrival, they learn that the bodies of the recently dead are going missing from their graves. It becomes clear that a wealthy squire named Clive Hamilton (John Carson) has been reviving the dead using voodoo rites he learned during his travels in Haiti. The aristocrat has been killing off the villagers and resurrecting them as zombies. They slave away (albeit slowly and extremely inefficiently) on a chain gang in Hamilton's recently condemned tin mines until a fiery uprising causes them to attack their master.

Shot back-to-back with *The Reptile* (also by Gilling), *Plague* repurposes some of the sets from that film to great effect. Most notable is a spooky dream sequence in which the dead slowly rise from their graves in a cemetery, clawing at dirt in filthy robes—a motif that would later become commonplace in the zombie film. Another memorable scene involves a villager's wife rising from the dead and being decapitated right before her husband's very eyes. With its somewhat sentient, white-eyed, moldy zombies and disturbing resurrection scene, *Plague of the Zombies* went on to become hugely influential on horror cinema across the globe.

And let's not forget the Italians. Following the peplum/horror hybrid *War of the Zombies* (1964), two more zombie-themed movies emerged from Italy in 1965: Massimo Pupillo's *Terror-Creatures from the Grave* and the Spanish/Italian co-production *Planet of the Vampires* from Italian horror maestro Mario Bava. The former is an atmospheric gothic-horror entry starring Barbara Steele, while the latter is a sci-fi trip to a planet of, well, vampires. The title is a misnomer as the creatures are actually zombies—reanimated corpses under the control of an alien force. It had a profound influence on *Alien* (1979), which cribs much of *Planet's* plot and style, but replaces the "vampires" with a race of bug-like xenomorphs with acid for blood.

But it was an Italian/American co-production shot one year earlier that would have the biggest influence on the future of zombie cinema. Based on the influential novel *I Am Legend* by Richard Matheson, *The Last Man on Earth* stars a miscast Vincent Price as Robert Morgan, a scientist who has survived a plague that has wiped out the planet's population and left behind a handful of bloodthirsty vampires. By day Robert roams the streets of Rome (standing in for L.A.) freely collecting supplies and killing sleeping vampires. But by night, the creatures terrorize Robert as they call out his name in an attempt to coax him out of his barricaded home. His dreadful existence involves daily drives to a fiery plague pit where he dumps his fresh kills, as well as having to endure the cries and pleas of his turned friends, neighbors and, agonizingly, even his dead wife. It's a grim portrait of American suburbia turned into an apocalyptic wasteland. At the film's finale, Robert is besieged by a newly formed order of surviving humanity that he's been mistakenly staking for full-on vampires. Morgan, being the only person with a natural immunity, is established as the real monster of the post-apocalyptic world and is gunned down for his sins.

Though they are referred to as vampires, the resurrected creatures in *The Last Man on Earth* are interchangeable with zombies, which is

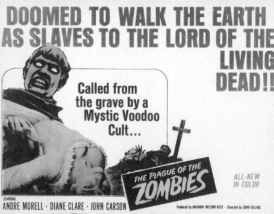

CLOCKWISE FROM ABOVE:
Local doctor Peter Tompson (Brook Williams), his old medical school professor Sir James Frobes (André Morell), and his daughter Sylvia (Diane Clare) begin to discover the bodies of the townspeople, in *The Plague of the Zombies* (1966).

A rich aristocrat uses voodoo to kill and revive the townspeople of Cornwall in *Plague of the Zombies*.

Zombies claw their way out of graves in *Plague of the Zombies*.

The most influential zombie film to come out of Britain in the 1960s.

exactly what George Romero did four years later with *Night of the Living Dead*. *The Last Man on Earth* was the first of three film adaptations of *I Am Legend*, including the Charlton Heston-led *Omega Man* (1971) and the abhorrent 2007 Will Smith star vehicle of the same name—none of which successfully captures the bleak, emotionally devastating tone of Matheson's seminal novel.

ABOVE CLOCKWISE FROM TOP LEFT:
Italy's first zombie film from 1964.

Terror-Creatures from the Grave (1965):
An atmospheric gothic-horror entry from Italy starring Barbara Steele.

Mario Bava's *Planet of the Vampires* (1965) features a space crew that

lands on a planet inhabited by
an alien force that possesses
the corpses of the team.

The Last Man on Earth (1964):
This American/Italian co-production would have a profound influence on zombie cinema, specifically George Romero's *Night of the Living Dead*.

CHAPTER 3

ROMERO'S FLESH-EATER RENAISSANCE & SPANISH ZOMBIES OF THE 1970S

Night of the Living Dead

As the UK and other countries experimented with making the zombie scary, most of the filmmakers in the United States during the 1960s demonstrated they didn't really know what a zombie was at all. That is, until a tiny little movie called *Night of the Living Dead* came along at the end of the decade and changed everything.

Cribbing a little from films such as *Invasion of the Body Snatchers* (1956), *Invisible Invaders* (1959), *The Earth Dies Screaming* (1965), *The Last Man on Earth* (1964), and a lot from Richard Matheson's seminal vampire apocalypse novel *I Am Legend* (1954), George Romero's *Night of the Living Dead* is perhaps the most famous, successful, and revered zombie picture of all time. It is the granddaddy of zombie apocalypse films, and it comes to us not from Hollywood, but Pittsburgh, Pennsylvania, of all places. In fact, it was the first feature ever produced in Pittsburgh—now known as the "zombie capital of the world."

Released on October 2, 1968, *Night of the Living Dead* tells the story of a diverse group of people who are under siege in a rural Pennsylvania farmhouse near a cemetery during a mysterious apocalypse that is causing the dead to rise and attack the living. On a visit to their father's grave, siblings Barbra (Judith O'Dea) and Johnny (Russell Streiner) encounter a ghoul (Bill Hinzman) who attacks and kills Johnny. Barbra escapes to an isolated farmhouse, where she is joined by Ben (Duane Jones), who barricades them inside. They are soon greeted by a group of people who have been hiding out in the cellar: young couple Tom (Keith Wayne) and Judy (Judith Ridley), and Harry and Helen Cooper (Karl Hardman and Marilyn Eastman) and their daughter Karen (Kyra Schon), who has been bitten by one of the attackers and fallen ill. Social order crumbles quickly as the group argues over who is in charge and whether or not they should barricade themselves in the cellar or fortify the house.

According to newscasts, the dead have been rising up all over the eastern seaboard and consuming the flesh of the living, but no one has any idea why or what can be done about it. It is only briefly hinted that perhaps high levels of radiation brought back from a Venus space probe is the culprit, but it is never explored further. (According to Romero, the distributor would not release the film until the filmmakers added some sort of an explanation for the phenomenon.) It is clear, however, that the dead can be "de-animated" by destroying the brain.

Before long, the individuals in the group turn on each other, increasing the level of paranoia, tension, claustrophobia, and helplessness. Tom and Judy are killed in a botched attempt to escape while fueling a truck (their barbequed remains become a snack for the ghouls), and cowardly businessman Harry tries to lock Ben out of the house. In the ensuing struggle, Harry is shot and killed. Helen later discovers her daughter Karen has been transformed into one of the ghouls when she finds her eating her father's remains. Karen brutally murders her mother with a garden trowel before she heads upstairs, where zombies have broken into the house. Barbra is dragged away by her now-undead brother and Ben retreats to the basement where he shoots the reanimated corpses of Harry and Helen and waits out the hordes until morning. When Ben emerges from the house the next day he is mistaken for a ghoul by a posse of trigger-happy police, militia, and rednecks, and he is quickly shot in the head. The film concludes with a disturbing montage of still photographs depicting Ben's body being

OPPOSITE: **Barbra (Judith O'Dea) and her brother Johnny (Russell Streiner) are attacked by a ghoul (Bill Hinzman) while visiting their father's grave in** *Night of the Living Dead* **(1968).**

dragged by hooks to a pyre where the dead are being incinerated.

All of this proved to be too much for critics in the late sixties. *Night* was lashed upon its release for being too gruesome—boldly depicting the ghouls gorging themselves on human entrails, tearing meat off of long bones (actually cooked ham), and even a little girl cannibalizing her own parents. *Variety* called the film an "unrelieved orgy of sadism," which only helped usher more young people to drive-ins and midnight screenings. *Night* grossed some $12 million domestically and $30 million internationally and, in 1999, it was selected by the Library of Congress for preservation in the National Film Registry as a film deemed "culturally, historically, or aesthetically significant."

Night was produced by Image Ten Corporation, a production company comprised of television commercial types including co-founder George Romero. The company wanted to move into feature films and landed on an idea from Romero that was based on *I Am Legend*. (When asked where Romero got the idea for *Night of the Living Dead*, he often replies, "I stole it, from Richard Matheson.") He borrowed the survivalist angle of the story and replaced the vampires with "ghouls"—non-supernatural creatures that rob graves and consume human flesh.

Unlike the zombies of movie cinema past, Romero's ghouls are not controlled by a mad scientist, alien intelligence, or voodoo practitioner. Rather, these undead cannibals lumber about slowly and purposefully in a

singular pursuit: food. Their clothing is a little ripped and their complexion a little raccoon-like, but they are definitely not past their expiration date. In other words, these zombies look like regular people—mostly. They retain some sense of self-preservation because they don't like being set on fire, and they clearly do possess some sense of memory and rudimentary intelligence because they use clubs and rocks to get to people, and in one instance even try to open a car door by its handle. And for whatever reason, they can only be de-animated by destroying the brain.

Although the creatures in *Night of the Living Dead* are never specifically referred to as "zombies," the movie ended up redefining the zombie subgenre and having a massive influence on the modern pop-culture zombie archetype.

Put simply, *Night of the Living Dead* gave the zombie its notorious "appetite" for destruction. The concept of the zombie as cannibal was unheard of until this point in cinema history. From this moment on, zombies would almost always be cannibals.

Though *Night* has been ruthlessly analyzed as having deep political subtext, Romero admits much of that can be chalked up to serendipity. For example, the script was already written before the filmmakers knew the character of Duane would be a black man. As it turns out, he was simply the best actor among his friends. So the intense racial subtext that arises in the film is entirely accidental. Similarly, much of the story was dictated by finances, rather than creative impetus. Romero stretched the film's

ABOVE: ***Night of the Living Dead*** was taboo for many reasons in 1968, including the brazen use of naked ghouls in the shoot.

$114,000 budget by shooting on black-and-white 35mm film and constraining most of the action to one location—just as Terrence Fisher did with *The Earth Dies Screaming*—and casting local unknown actors. Its low budget imbued the film with a documentary, or *cinéma vérité*, esthetic similar to wartime newsreels of the day. Whether or not the filmmakers had deliberately planned it, the result was a contemporary horror film that was subversive on many levels, but chiefly as a critique of American authority and its involvement in the Vietnam War.

What Romero and company did intentionally with *Night of the Living Dead* is push the envelope of modern horror with its dead serious, taboo-breaking tone, deeply flawed "hero," and bleak ending. There are no romantic subplots or

moments of comic relief; dominant ideological values are reasserted at the end of the movie, but order is definitely not restored. Things are clearly not better than they were before. In fact, the nation is under collapse and it appears there is increasing chaos, relentless nihilism and violence—on the part of the human survivors. Like Alfred Hitchcock's *Psycho*, *Night* places the terror in the home, between family members, blurring the line between the monstrous and the ordinary. In this case, the ordinary becomes monstrous. As Romero is so fond of saying, "They're the neighbors . . . they're us."

ABOVE: **Although the creatures in *Night of the Living Dead* were never explicitly referred to as "zombies," the film redefined the zombie subgenre forever. From this point on, the undead would almost always be depicted as hungry for human flesh.**

All images courtesy Robert L. Lucas.

The 1970s

Following the release of *Night of the Living Dead* in 1968, the zombie seemed to have a new lease on un-life as the next decade saw a horde of zombie films emerge from the growing international exploitation scene. By this time, Europe, Hong Kong, and even Bollywood were catching on to the zombie craze, in part thanks to the success of Hammer's *The Plague of the Zombies* (1966) in those markets. Nevertheless, the zombie was still finding its footing at the beginning of the decade with the release of bizarre British undead biker movies such as *Psychomania* (1971) and trashy, unwatchable Mexican Boris Karloff vehicles such as *The Snake People* (1971). It wasn't really until Spanish director Amando de Ossorio shot the first in a series of Knights Templar–themed zombie films that the monster really rose to popularity overseas.

De Ossorio's quartet of zombie films—which comprises *Tombs of the Blind Dead* (1971), *The Return of the Blind Dead* (1973), *The Ghost Galleon* (1974), and *Night of the Sea Gulls* (1975)—featured unstoppable, blind zombie monks on ghost horses pursuing their prey by sound alone. The series begins with *Tombs* (a.k.a. *La noche del terror ciego*), about a trio of travelers—Betty (Lone Fleming), Virginia (María Elena Arpón), and Roger (César Burner)—who are journeying across the Portuguese countryside by rail when Virginia detrains in a fit of jealously. Evidently Roger is interested in her friend Betty, with whom she had a lesbian affair years ago. She accidentally stumbles upon the resting place of the Knights Templar, a sect of thirteenth-century, devil-worshipping monks who were hanged almost a thousand years ago for sacrificing virgins and drinking their blood in pursuit of eternal life. For their unholy deeds, the Templars' corpses were left to have their eyes pecked out by crows.

Deciding the creepy, crumbling monastery is a good place to bed for the night, Virginia lays

DIE NACHT DER REITENDEN LEICHEN

OPPOSITE: **Spanish director Amando de Ossorio reinvented the zombie in 1971 with *Tombs of the Blind Dead*. Pictured here is the Italian poster for the film.**

CLOCKWISE FROM TOP LEFT:
Director Amando de Ossorio with one of his undead Templar Knights. Image courtesy Blue Undergound.

Blind skeletal monks terrorize the living on ghostly horseback in *Tombs of the Blind Dead* (1971). Image courtesy Blue Underground.

The blind monks chase an escapee to a train where they slaughter everyone on board. Image courtesy Blue Underground.

out her sleeping gear, strips to her underwear, and goes to sleep. This awakens the monks, who chase her around the grounds in a protracted orgy of blood drinking. When she does not return the next day, her friends enlist the help of a couple of local smugglers (huh?) and go looking for her. The moldy monks eventually kill off everyone save for Betty. The film climaxes when the Templars board a train and kill everyone on

board—children included—establishing an open-ended apocalypse scenario, in which the zombies spread their terror to neighboring towns and, possibly, beyond.

Like many European exploitation films of the era, *Tombs of the Blind Dead* is a decidedly sexist entry that includes rituals involving naked female virgins who watch as their breasts are mutilated,

a shameless rape scene in which the male smuggler tries to convert Betty to heterosexuality by force, and even a lesbian subplot, added to give the director a reason to shoot a scene in which Betty and Virginia roll around in bed together. As chauvinistic as they are, these elements were characteristic of the growing Eurotic horror movement—a series of sleazy and sometimes X-rated movies that combined sex with horror to appease the raincoat crowd, which was currently enjoying mainstream porn films such as *Deep Throat* (1972) in theaters. In Europe, onscreen sex was becoming much more hardcore, and the horror movie responded in kind by amping up the sleaze factor. This gave birth to a glittery new wave of sexploitation horror films from directors like Jean Rollin (*The Nude Vampire*, 1970), Jess Franco (*A Virgin Among the Living Dead*, 1973), Andrea Bianchi (*Strip Nude for Your Killer*, 1975), and Joe D'Amato (*Erotic Nights of the Living Dead*, 1980).

Rollin's *The Grapes of Death* (1978) is one of the better zombie films to come out of the Eurotic horror cycle. Its zombies are diseased, violent people, rather than undead corpses, prefiguring *28 Days Later*'s "infected" by more than two decades.

Some critics have indicated the *Blind Dead* series as being subversive commentaries on the repressive Franco regime, with the Templar Knights summoned from the grave at the start of each film as a way of representing the old values of Spain rising up against the youth of the day. This makes sense, but the presupposition is that excessive nubile female flesh being mauled by dead hands serves to stand in for our own mortality, and excuses the rampant misogyny in de Ossorio's quadrilogy. It's much more reasonable to just accept such scenes for what they are: evidence of the ever-present chauvinist male gaze in European horror cinema.

ABOVE LEFT AND TOP: **Rare concept art for *Return of the Blind Dead* (1973), the sequel to *Tombs of the Blind Dead*. Images courtesy Blue Underground.**

ABOVE: **Undead gang rape is rampant in *The Ghost Galleon* (1974), the third entry in Amando de Ossorio's *Blind Dead* series. Image courtesy Blue Underground.**

While still nowhere near as sexually extreme and misogynistic as the rest of the Eurotic horror movement, *Tombs* is a refreshing, if tasteless, take on the zombie genre with its spooky, skeletal zombie knights in rotting shrouds galloping about like the Four Horseman of the Apocalypse. It's a decisively slow, but lyrical, stylish, and atmospheric zombie film aided by a wonderful Gothic soundtrack from Antón García-Abril, who uses haunting monastic chanting to great effect. Finally, *Tombs* is set against a lush backdrop and employs slow-motion photography in a way the world has never seen; watching a renegade band of dusty undead Satanic priests on ghostly horseback is truly a sight to behold.

Director de Ossorio has always insisted his blind killer priests weren't zombies at all, but mummies. Regardless, his *Blind Dead* films were hugely influential and gave rise to the most significant Spanish zombie movie of the

1970s: Catalonian director Jorge Grau's *Let Sleeping Corpses Lie* (a.k.a. *The Living Dead at Manchester Morgue, Don't Open the Window*, 1974), a film that bridged the gap between Romero's *Night of the Living Dead* and his later splatter sequel, *Dawn of the Dead* (1978). According to Grau, the film's producers wanted him to shoot a retooling of *Night of the Living Dead* but in color. What he delivered was a surprisingly gory zombie film with an ecological message that presaged the ultra-bloody Italian zombie cycle of the 1980s.

Despite the movie's alternate title, the story takes place in the bucolic town of Windermere in Northern England's Lake District. The Experimental Section of the government's Agricultural Department has developed a new machine that uses ultrasonic waves and radiation for pest extermination by controlling the nervous systems of primitive creatures. The machine does a good job of making

ABOVE LEFT: **German Poster for Amando de Ossorio's *The Ghost Galleon* (1974). Image courtesy Blue Underground.**

ABOVE: **Sex and horror frolicked in the same stained bed for Jean Rollin's *Grapes of Death* (1978), one of the better films in the Eurotic horror cycle.**

grasshoppers kill each other during testing, but unfortunately it has two minor drawbacks: it causes babies to act homicidal and also resurrects the recently dead.

Suddenly a rash of murders afflict the town and the bigoted local police sergeant (Arthur Kennedy) suspects two out-of-towners: sculptress Edna (Cristina Galbó) and cranky antique dealer George (Ray Lovelock), who have been traveling together since Edna backed her car into George's motorcycle at a gas station. The ravenous dead soon take over the town and the lawman pretty much lets it happen, refusing to believe anyone other than the hippie in the "faggot clothes" could be responsible. The film climaxes when the sergeant shoots George dead after he rescues (an already turned) Edna from a horde of corpses about to be shipped to the Manchester morgue. She is set ablaze

in a scene that almost elicits sympathy in the viewer as Edna reaches her arms out in fear while she burns. In an act of poetic justice, George is eventually reanimated by the machine and takes revenge on the policeman.

The similarities to *Night of the Living Dead* are obvious. *Let Sleeping Corpses Lie* posits a non-supernatural (environmental catastrophe) source of the plague and also presents law enforcement as cruel, brutish, and reactionary. But this English language, Italian/Spanish co-production is no mere remake of Romero's film. The zombies are much more hostile, a little more intelligent, and can't be killed by destroying the brain. (Fire is pretty much the only thing that takes these bad boys out.) In a curious supernatural twist, older corpses can be reanimated by the recently resurrected in a ritual that involves placing a drop of blood in the eyes of the cadaver. But what makes the

ABOVE LEFT: **The Spanish poster for Jorge Grau's *Let Sleeping Corpses Lie* (a.k.a. *The Living Dead at Manchester Morgue*, *Don't Open the Window*, 1974).**

TOP: **The recently deceased are revived through an environmental catastrophe in *Let Sleeping Corpses Lie*. Unlike Romero's ghouls, these zombies can only be destroyed with fire. Image courtesy Blue Underground.**

ABOVE: **Ray Lovelock plays George, the unwitting zombie hero in *Let Sleeping Corpses Lie*.**

film most unique is that that it asks the viewer to identify with the zombies (George and Edna, specifically). For the first time in cinema history, audiences found themselves rooting for the zombie hero at the end of *Let Sleeping Corpses Lie* as he takes revenge against the lawman who wronged him.

Elsewhere in Spain, Paul Naschy (that country's answer to Lon Chaney Jr.) was busy ripping off classic horror by appearing as a variety of Universal-inspired monsters including a hunchback, a mummy, and Count Dracula. His most popular series revolved around a wolfman named Waldemar Daninsky, a character he played in twelve different films. But in 1973, Naschy (real name Jacinto Molina) appeared in a trio of lowball zombie titles: *Vengeance of the Zombies*, *Return of the Zombies*, and *Horror Rises from the Tomb*. In the films, he plays an East Indian voodoo practitioner, a necrophilic gravedigger, and a fifteenth-century Satanist, respectively. All three were tedious, poorly received, and proved that Naschy's best work didn't involve zombies.

The Spanish may have ruled the zombie film market in the 1970s, but that didn't stop the Brits from churning out a handful of mostly missable living dead films. *Neither the Sea nor the Sand* (1972) is a depressing romantic fantasy about a woman whose lover dies and returns as a zombie. Though it plays out something like *Ghost* with a zombie lover, the film has absolutely no pulse whatsoever. *Disciple of Death* (1972) is a British cheapie about an eighteenth-century Satanist who returns to life after a droplet of virgin blood lands on his tomb. Amateur production values and worse acting plague the film, which pretty much disappeared into obscurity. Fortunately, horror anthology pioneer Amicus Studios was on hand to deliver some classic thrills with *Tales from the Crypt* (1972), a collection of five chilling stories based on the EC comic of the same name. Of particular note is the zombie-themed segment entitled "Poetic Justice," starring Peter Cushing as a widower who gets some undead revenge

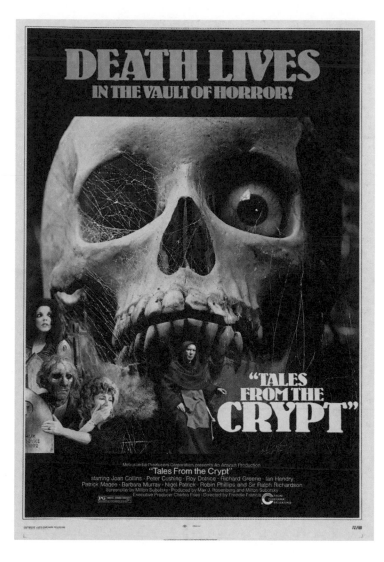

against the neighbors who framed and drove him to suicide. Cushing also appears alongside Christopher Lee and Telly Savalas in the following year's *Horror Express*, about a cranky frozen space zombie that thaws out on board a trans-Siberian express train. As silly as it sounds, *Horror Express* is one of the better zombie films to come out of the UK during the decade. *Horror Hospital* (1973), on the other hand, is a completely forgettable remote-control zombie film in the vein of *The Phantom of the Paradise*. Hammer Studios also weighed in with a bizarre UK/Hong Kong collaboration called *The Legend of the 7 Golden Vampires* (1973). The tale, which

ABOVE: *Tales from the Crypt*: **This Amicus anthology features a rather chilling zombie-themed short entitled "Poetic Justice," starring Peter Cushing.**

plays out like Dracula goes to the Orient, was a flop and ended up being one of the last horror films the studio would produce.

Back on American soil, filmgoers were faring a little bit better—excusing Al Adamson's downright inept and irredeemable zombie outing *Blood of Ghastly Horror* (1972), of course. Thankfully, at the same time writer/filmmaker duo Alan Ormsby and Bob Clark teamed up for their first collaboration on a humorous low-budget zombie flick called *Children Shouldn't Play with Dead Things* (1972).

Shot in Florida on a budget of $70,000, *Children* is a campy, bloody, and frequently funny drive-in classic about a group of actors who are rehearsing for a play on a remote island when their director (co-writer/star Alan Ormsby) decides they're going to raise the dead. They dig up a corpse dubbed "Orville" and use it as part of a Satanic ritual inscribed in an old book (an influence on Sam Raimi's *The Evil Dead* perhaps?). Before they know it, the jackoffs are locked inside a shed that's besieged by zombies, in a scenario that's clearly inspired by *Night of the Living Dead*. While the film is far from perfect, it's one of the first horror comedies that featured flesh-eating zombies—which sadly don't appear until the last thirty minutes of the film. But it rises above the average zom-com in that it pokes fun at the failed hippie movement and puts emphasis on the disillusionment many were feeling in the 1970s.

Politics take center stage in Clark and Ormsby's next film, the ultra-creepy "Monkey's Paw" tale, *Deathdream* (1974). For *Deathdream* (a.k.a. *Dead of Night* and *The Night Andy Came Home*), the pair managed to source a budget five times the size of *Children* from that film's Canadian distributor. Young G.I. Andy Brooks has gone off to fight in the Vietnam War but hasn't been heard from in weeks. His father and sister are convinced he's dead, but his mother obsessively prays for his safe return and when he appears, his family is overjoyed. But something is different about Andy (Richard Backus), who spends most of his time rocking in a chair in the darkened attic, wearing sunglasses at

night and generally creeping his family out. As the film progresses, Andy's mysterious affliction progresses too, as his eyes sink further into his skull and he turns violent. After he kills the family dog in front of his father (played by *The Godfather*'s John Marley), the family degenerates into loud, alcohol-fueled screaming matches.

It turns out Andy is a blood-drinking zombie who must feed on human plasma in order to keep his rapidly decomposing body from completely rotting out (courtesy make-up by

ABOVE: **The Spanish poster for the UK's *Horror Express*, an unusual zombie film about a frozen monster that thaws out aboard a train.**

Ormsby and a fresh-from-Vietnam-himself Tom Savini). In a series of genuinely creepy scenes, he attempts to drink the blood of a physician and even his girlfriend until the heartbreaking and poignant ending in which Andy tries to bury himself in a grave.

By this point in zombie cinema it's clear that *Night of the Living Dead* did more for the creature than simply resurrect it. *Night* proved that zombie films could have style and subversive subtext that reflected topical social anxieties. *Deathdream* is a strong example of such a film, as it challenged the establishment with its overt critique of the Vietnam War. No solider ever returns home from war the same, and no family is ever unaffected by it. *Deathdream* tragically reminded parents of a disillusioned generation to be careful what they wished for. Superlative and essential viewing.

Critiquing the prevailing social order was a common thread throughout zombie-themed films of the 1970s. Though not zombie films proper, *Let's Scare Jessica to Death* (1972), *Messiah of Evil* (1973), *Garden of the Dead* (1974), Romero's *The Crazies* (1973), David Cronenberg's *Shivers* (1975), and Jeff Lieberman's *Blue Sunshine* (1977) all feature either hippies, prisoners, or regular people turned into homicidal maniacs via either chemical contagion, drug use, or biological infection. These films are dominated by themes of family and friends revealing their strangeness and attempting to recruit others into that strangeness. By the beginning of the 1970s, the hippie dream was a thing of the past, and these films illustrated that social angst expertly—especially *Shivers*, which punishes the liberated inhabitants of a high rise with an STD that turns people into frothy-mouthed, sex-crazed maniacs.

Of course, not every zombie-themed movie that emerged in the States during the 1970s was a thinking-person's film, political allegory, or even a good movie for that matter. Mimes, children, afro'd barmaids, and even Nazis all got the zombie treatment in the "Me-generation" decade. In 1974 *The House of Seven Corpses* and

IT WRINGS THE VICTIMS OUT.. AND HANGS THEM UP TO DIE!!!

DEATHDREAM

STARRING: JOHN MARLEY · LYNN CARLIN WITH: RICHARD BACKUS · HENDERSON FORSYTH
Screenplay Written by: ALAN ORMSBY Music by: CARL ZITTRER Executive Producers: JOHN TRENT & PETER JAMES
Produced and Directed by: BOB CLARK

A QUADRANT IMPACT FILM [PG] PARENTAL GUIDANCE SUGGESTED Color by: TECHNICOLOR
An ENTERTAINMENT INTERNATIONAL PICTURES RELEASE DEATHDREAM-76/195

The House on Skull Mountain were released. The former is a dull, nonsensical, padded-out film starring John Carradine, and the latter is an equally slow, voodoo-themed blaxploitation effort from Twentieth Century Fox. Then there's William Castle's *Shanks* (1974), a wacky comedy starring world-famous mime Marcel Marceau as a deaf mute puppeteer who controls the undead with the help of a mad scientist (also played by Marceau!). It was the last film Castle directed before his passing in 1977. Viewers would be better off watching one of his better-known titles, such as *The House on Haunted Hill* (1959).

ABOVE: **Richard Backus stars as Andy Brooks, an undead G.I. who returns from the Vietnam War as a blood-drinking zombie, in *Deathdream*.**

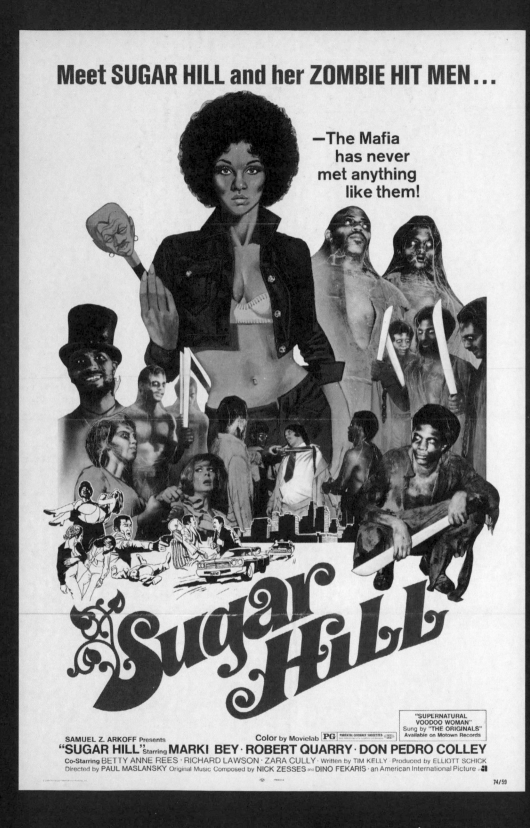

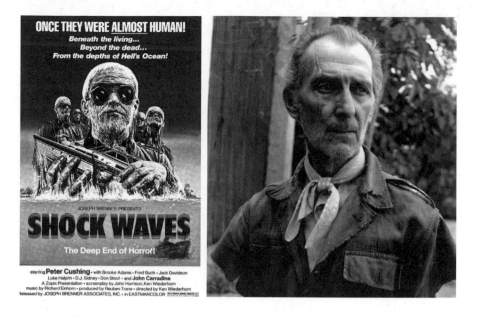

ONCE THEY WERE **ALMOST HUMAN!**
Beneath the living...
Beyond the dead...
From the depths of Hell's Ocean!

JOSEPH BRENNER PRESENTS

SHOCK WAVES
The Deep End of Horror!

starring **Peter Cushing** · with Brooke Adams · Fred Buch · Jack Davidson
Luke Halprin · D.J. Sidney · Don Stout · and **John Carradine**
A Zopix Presentation · screenplay by John Harrison, Ken Wiederhorn
music by Richard Einhorn · produced by Reuben Trane · directed by Ken Wiederhorn
Released by JOSEPH BRENNER ASSOCIATES, INC. · in EASTMANCOLOR

"Meet SUGAR HILL and her ZOMBIE HIT MEN . . . The Mafia has never met anything like them!" So goes the humorous tagline for blaxploitation effort *Sugar Hill* (1974), a film that admittedly does possess some political subtext that is mostly ignored in favor of distractions such as an attacking, severed chicken claw, outrageously loud clothing, and wicked seventies' 'fros. Nightclub owner Diana Hill (Marki Bey), a.k.a. "Sugar," enlists the help of a voodoo practitioner to get revenge against the unruly white suckas who brutally murdered her boyfriend. The closest the film gets to racial commentary is through the use of former slaves from Guinea who died in the 1840s and were buried in a New Orleans swamp. Otherwise this jive turkey is a revenge film, straight up. Oh, and keep an eye out for Robert Quarry (a.k.a. Count Yorga) as the gang leader!

Not even soft-core pornographer Harry Novak (*Booby Trap*) could resist making a zombie movie toward the end of his career. *The Child* (1977) is a thankfully non-pornographic snorefest inspired by Karen, the matricidal moppet from *Night of the Living Dead*. A psychic eleven-year-old named Rosalie (Rosalie Cole) with the power to raise the dead uses the monsters against anyone who angers her. This messy but creepy movie probably owes more to *The Omen* than *Night of the Living Dead*, but it's not the last time children and zombies would intersect in horror cinema.

Everyone knows *Shock Waves* (1977) as that "nazi zombie movie" with the freaky, goggled Toten Korps. This low-budget sleeper updates the evil nazi zombie motif with sometimes eerie results. A group of boating tourists (led by horror stalwart John Carradine) becomes stranded on an island inhabited by a former Nazi officer (Peter Cushing) and his army of waterlogged undead SS soldiers. The death squad, engineered in the Second World War to man U-boats, never have to come up for air. Nazi scientists chose "cheap hoodlums, thugs, and a good number of pathological murderers and sadists" as test subjects. Of course, the crew went berzerk and Cushing sank the ship, leaving them squatting off the coast of Florida (?) until now. It's a slow burn, but it's worth the watch for some truly unnerving scenes of Nazi zombies rising out of the sea and making their way to shore. *Shock Waves* may also be the only horror film that contains a death by sea urchin. It also features creepy, leathery skinned make-up by Alan Ormsby (*Children Shouldn't Play with Dead Things*, *Deathdream*) and atmospheric direction by Ken Wiederhorn, who later directed *Return of the Living Dead II*.

OPPOSITE: **Blaxploitation and zombies collide in 1974's *Sugar Hill*.**

ABOVE LEFT: **Poster for *Shock Waves* (1977), starring the freaky Toten Korps. Image courtesy Blue Underground.**

ABOVE: **Peter Cushing as a former Nazi commander in *Shock Waves*. Image courtesy Blue Underground.**

Dawn of the Dead

The European zombie ruled the roost until 1978, when an American zombie film with Italian connections was released that changed the subgenre forever. Ten years after *Night of the Living Dead*, George Romero shot *Martin* (1977), a contemporary vampire film that put the filmmaker back on the horror map. He was then approached by Italian director Dario Argento (*Suspiria*, *Deep Red*) to produce a sequel to *Night*. Under the terms of their agreement, Romero would write and direct, while Argento consulted with a view to produce an extra violent version for the European market, bankrolled by his brother and film producer Claudio Argento. The Argentos knew their target audience and insisted the film's score should be composed by Italian prog-rockers Goblin, whom both had worked with previously.

ABOVE: **Theatrical poster for *Dawn of the Dead*, the most significant zombie film of the 1970s.**

Though the film he ended up making has often been cited as a deliberate commentary on consumerism, as it features zombies shambling around a mall in an undead mental daze still shopping for things they no longer need, the truth is, it actually kind of happened by accident. Around that time, Romero had met a group that developed an indoor shopping mall in Pittsburgh, complete with attic crawl spaces stocked with Civil Defense supplies—escape in case of nuclear attack. It gave him an idea for a sequel, finally.

Romero's line of thinking concluded with another politically inclined siege film where a group of people are holed up, just in a bigger place—and with much more gore and violence than its predecessor. After all, the world had changed markedly in the intervening years between *Night* and *Dawn* as a result of the Vietnam War; violence was everywhere. When the mall came into the picture, it allowed him

the opportunity to imbue the movie with a satirical commentary on social consumption (of several kinds), so he locked himself up in a Rome hotel room and penned the script for what would become the legendary *Dawn of the Dead*.

The story picks up immediately after the events of *Night of the Living Dead*. The zombie apocalypse is in full swing and a couple—the employees of a television station—Fran (Gaylen Ross) and her pilot boyfriend Stephen (David Emge), decide to make a run for safety in the news helicopter. They are joined by SWAT team members Peter (Ken Foree) and Roger (Scott H. Reiniger) after a failed attempt to contain a violent outbreak in a Puerto Rican tenement whose inhabitants refused to hand over their dead for incineration. The four eventually land on the roof of a shopping mall, where they are safe after clearing out the undead loitering around in it, until a gang of bikers (led by

Tom Savini in a famous role) break in, bringing the zombie horde with them. Stephen and Roger are bitten; Fran and Peter climb to the roof and narrowly escape in the helicopter, which is low on fuel.

According to Romero, the original ending saw Peter and a pregnant Fran commit suicide via self-inflicted gunshot and helicopter-blade decapitation, respectively, but the filmmaker felt it was far too bleak (and the decapitation not quite good enough) and only filmed portions of it, though none of it has ever been released to the public. Though the movie suffers from some poor pacing, ridiculous blue-skinned zombies, and a tin ear for dialog, no one had seen an exploding head or an eviscerated person done quite so graphically before *Dawn of the Dead* (courtesy of Savini). Romero decided to avoid the MPAA (who would have surely slapped it with an X rating) and released the film unrated. It was a gamble that earned the film over $55 million worldwide (it was made for $650,000), proving there was a huge new market for a gory thinking-person's zombie film, and at the same time kicking off a new era of hyper-violence in genre cinema. *Dawn* was particularly successful in Italy, where Argento released it with less dialog and comedy before it even hit theaters in the United States. That version quickly spawned a legion of imitators that eventually formed an entire subgenre of Italian zombie films.

RIGHT TOP TO BOTTOM:
The infamous exploding head in *Dawn of the Dead* (1978).

A zombified Stephen (David Emge) leads the horde to the survivors' secret crawlspace in the mall.

***Dawn of the Dead* established zombie characters such as the "Plaid Shirt Zombie" and the "Nurse Zombie."**

Lucio Fulci's *Zombie*

From *The Ten Commandments* to *Star Wars*, scores of westerns, James Bond flicks, and even *Jaws*, the Italians were remaking almost every successful American movie they could get away with during the seventies—and *Dawn of the Dead* was no exception. When it was released in Italy in 1978 as *Zombi* (Italian for zombie, obviously), journeyman film director Lucio Fulci decided to capitalize on its success by making his own gore-filled zombie entry in the long tradition of Italian copycat films. To further advance the illusion, a legal loophole allowed him to slap a sequel number on an existing title (*Zombi*), as though it were actually a follow-up to *Dawn*. Shameless but true.

Fulci's knock-off was called *Zombi 2,* and while it was designed to be a copy of *Dawn* right down to its tagline ("When the earth spits out the dead . . . They will return to tear the flesh of the living"), the director claimed his zombies were more inspired by Jacques Tourneur's *I Walked with a Zombie* than Romero's ghouls. A less partial evaluation of the film reveals a bit of both, though. *Zombie* takes place in the Caribbean, where the creature was born, and it also exudes the (however unintentional) racial overtones characteristic of early voodoo-themed zombie films. But the flesh-eating element is pure Romero. That said, the way Fulci executed the gore was groundbreaking and ended up defining the rest of his horror filmmaking career.

The film begins when an abandoned ocean yacht carrying an overweight zombie drifts into the New York harbor. Once on the scene, police are attacked by the portly stiff and forced to shoot it down. The daughter of the vessel's owner (Anne Bowles, played by Tisa Farrow) teams up with investigative reporter Peter West (Ian McCulloch), and they sail to the Caribbean island of Matul to search for Anne's father. Accompanied by two friends from whom they charter a boat (Brian and Susan, played by Al Cliver and Auretta Gay), they make their way across the cannibal zombie–infested tropical paradise. Along the way viewers are treated to a near-naked scuba diving scene, a gushing throat-ripping, a downright merciless eye-splintering that will have you squirming in disgust, and even an unbelievable underwater shark vs. zombie fight! The film culminates in a dreary scenario in which the undead can be seen roaming the Brooklyn Bridge, setting itself up as a prequel to *Dawn of the Dead*.

TOP: **The U.S. theatrical poster for Zombie (1979), Lucio Fulci's gory knock-off of Dawn of the Dead.**

ABOVE: **An overweight zombie arrives in the New York harbor.**

As would become common in Fulci's horror films, the director eschews narrative logic in favor of nightmarish imagery in *Zombie*, which also suffers from terrible dubbing, wooden acting, low production values, and a threadbare plot. But as the late Chas. Balun would say, it sure brings home the gore groceries! Inspired by the outrageously gory and notorious cannibal cycle of the 1970s (*Deep River Savages*, *Last Cannibal World*, *Emanuelle and the Last Cannibals*), *Zombie* took the horror film to new heights of gruesomeness with nasty, Grand Guignol–style gore from Giannetto De Rossi (*The Living Dead at Manchester Morgue*). For most viewers, all that gore more than makes up for the lack of subtext.

With its corporeal, clay-faced zombies, exploitation elements, Goblin-esque score (from Fabio Frizzi), and atmospheric setting, *Zombie* proved to be more successful at the box office than its American predecessor. In fact, it remains one of the highest grossing Italian horror films of all time. Not surprisingly, an explosion of copycats ensued.

TOP: **Olga Karlatos is terrorized in an outrageously drawn-out scene in which a zombie pulls her toward a twelve-inch splinter that punctures her eye and breaks off in the socket.**

ABOVE LEFT TO RIGHT:
Director Lucio Fulci allegedly hired homeless people and winos as zombie extras or "walking flowerpots," as he called them.

A throat-ripping is just one of the nasty thrills on display in *Zombie*.

Inspired by the notoriously gory Italian cannibal films, *Zombie* used groundbreaking, corporeal make-up effects by Giannetto De Rossi.

The 1980s: The Era of the Italian Zombie

More zombie movies were produced during the 1980s than any other decade in history thanks in large part to the booming home-video market. In fact, the numbers are so staggering, it would be impossible to include them all here (see sidebar p. 99). A significant percentage of those movies were produced and filmed in Italy, with the rest made stateside, where horror had become the most commercially successful genre. It was the popular era of the "slasher film," and this meant everyone from genre royalty like John Carpenter to Z-listers like Bruno Mattei were cavorting with the living dead.

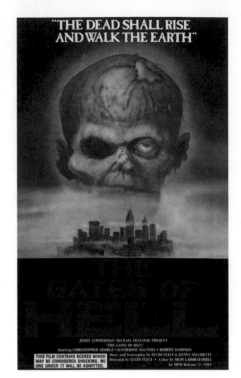

With Fulci's *Zombie* leading the way, a massive influx of Italian zombie movies flooded North America during the 1980s. For the most part, gone was any meaningful subtext, replaced by sensationalistic splatter and unabashed gore. The floodgates were about to open and Fulci himself was first in line with a series of three zombie-themed movies: *City of the Living Dead* (1980), *The Beyond* (1981), and *The House by the Cemetery* (1981). These films are the centerpiece of the Italian zombie film cycle and also represent Fulci's best work. They were conceived as a loose unholy trilogy, each involving the opening of one of seven gates of Hell and unleashing a living dead apocalypse on the world. Abandoning the influence of Romero, Fulci and screenwriter Dardano Sacchetti looked to the supernatural mythos of H. P. Lovecraft and the "Book of Revelation" as inspiration for this Gothic triptych of films.

City of the Living Dead (a.k.a. *The Gates of Hell*) takes place in the Lovecraftian town of Dunwich,

where a priest (Fabrizio Jovine) has opened one of the gates of Hell by hanging himself in a church graveyard. Fulci regular Catriona MacColl stars as Mary Woodhouse, a New York City psychic who has been having terrifying visions about Dunwich. Along with reporter Peter Bell (Christopher George), she travels to the sleepy town and tries to prevent the gates of Hell from opening permanently.

Shot entirely in New York with mostly Italian actors (including future *Cemetery Man* director Michele Soavi), *City of the Living Dead* suffers from the same flaws as much of Fulci's ouvre: bad dubbing, comical acting, and out-of-place dialog. These films are also characterized by oneiric logic that is too often misinterpreted by critics as ineptitude, when in fact outrageous gore sequences and doom-laden images are deliberately privileged above narrative coherence. With this trilogy in particular, Fulci refuses the conventional rules and structures of film, which results in a barrage of apocalyptic images that play out like some living nightmare.

TOP: **The U.S. poster for *City of the Living Dead* (a.k.a. *Gates of Hell*, 1980), the first in an unholy trinity of zombie films from Italian director Lucio Fulci.**

In terms of gore, *City of the Living Dead* is no slouch. Amazingly inventive death scenarios include a protracted shot of a lathe puncturing a skull and coming out the other side and a woman crying tears of blood while throwing up all of her small intestines; there's even an intense moment in which Peter rescues Mary from being buried alive with a pickaxe that comes alarmingly close to her skull as he drives it into her coffin lid. There is also plenty of brain-squeezing, torn flesh, and even raining maggots—not to mention a nonsensical ending that leaves audiences bewildered and at a loss for an explanation.

Confused viewers fared no better with *The Beyond*, an even more baffling and fractured story about a woman (Liza, played by MacColl) who inherits a rundown New Orleans hotel that was built over one of the seven entrances to Hell. A series of bizarre supernatural incidents plague the renovations of the building: a plumber and maid are murdered, an architect is attacked and eaten by (risibly

fake-looking) tarantulas, and the plumber's widow inexplicably becomes the victim of an acid facial while visiting her husband's corpse in the morgue. Later, a little zombie girl's head is ventilated by an exaggerated shotgun blast in a gore sequence from Giannetto De Rossi that went down as one of the most tastelessly nasty moments in Italian zombie movie history.

According to Fulci, *The Beyond* is an "absolute film"—one that is completely devoid of plot, where image and sound are of paramount importance. Assuredly unconventional, *The Beyond* is best interpreted as a gore-drenched art film with a (extremely) loose narrative about the nature of human existence. As the film reaches its climax, even rules dictated by time and space fall into nightmarish collapse as Liza and a hospital doctor (David Warbeck) face off against milky-eyed disappearing zombies from the beyond. Of course, it all ends badly for the protagonists as they barrel toward an unavoidable supernatural apocalypse.

TOP LEFT TO RIGHT: **Fulci's obsession with ocular trauma continues in** *City of the Living Dead* **with a victim who cries tears of blood prior to throwing up her own intestines.**

Fulci's vision of Hell in *The Beyond*.

ABOVE LEFT TO RIGHT: **Fulci's flesh-eaters like to squeeze brains rather than eat them in** *City of the Living Dead*. **Image courtesy Jay Slater.**

Gore effects from Giannetto De Rossi in *The Beyond* **include this scene in which a little zombie girl receives a shotgun blast to the head. Image courtesy Jay Slater.**

Fulci faces the law of diminishing returns in the final installment of the trilogy, *The House by the Cemetery*. Norman (Paolo Malco), his wife Lucy (MacColl again), and their son (Giovanni Frezza) move to a country house in Boston that—you guessed it—contains one of the gates of Hell. The former owner, nineteenth-century mad surgeon Dr. Freudstein, is now a zombie squatting in their basement, and the unwanted houseguest is causing some problems for the family, namely eating them. If the gushing mannequin neck and unexplained pools of blood weren't enough to stupefy audiences, the logic-defying ending definitely was. *House* was Fulci's least successful zombie film, grossing the equivalent of around $230,000. After *House*, Fulci abandoned the zombie subgenre and would not return to it until 1988 with the completely dismal *Zombi 3*. After Fulci fell ill, *Zombi 3* was completed by Bruno Mattei, who shoehorned in far too many unnecessary exposition scenes in a film that is memorable only for a hysterical sequence in which a zombie head launches itself out of a refrigerator. It would be Fulci's last zombie film before his passing. Incidentally, Claudio Fragasso's *Zombie 4: After Death* (1988) and Claudio

Lattanzi's *Killing Birds* (a.k.a. *Zombie 5*, 1987) have even less going for them—believe it or not.

Besides Fulci, there were plenty of other Italian directors attempting to capitalize on the success of *Zombie*. As would be expected from films that are copies of a rip-off, most of these titles never matched the quality of Fulci's work (and that's saying something given that Fulci is considered by many to be a hack director). Almost immediately, the popular Italian cannibal subgenre began to cross-pollinate with the zombie film in titles such as 1980's *Cannibal Apocalypse* (about a rabies-like virus that turns people into raging flesh-eaters) and *Zombie Holocaust* (a.k.a *Dr. Butcher, M.D.*, 1981), which borrows heavily from the previous year's *Cannibal Holocaust* but throws zombies and mad doctors into the mix. The former stars cult-icon John Saxon while the latter repurposes *Zombie*'s Ian McCulloch. Both are rather goofy time-wasters that appropriately abandon the realm of good taste in favor of titties and torture—and sometimes titty torture.

Other Italian directors pushed the limits of bad taste to the breaking point with zombie-themed

ABOVE LEFT: Nineteenth-century mad surgeon Dr. Freudstein, now a zombie, terrorizes a family in the final installment of Fulci's zombie trilogy, *The House by the Cemetery*.

ABOVE: Fulci returned to the zombie subgenre in 1988 with the abysmal *Zombie 3*, completed by director Bruno Mattei after Fulci fell ill. Image courtesy Jay Slater.

Their rabid lust for human flesh created an epidemic
EDMONDO AMATI PRESENTS **JOHN SAXON** IN
"INVASION OF THE FLESH HUNTERS"
WITH **ELIZABETH TURNER · JOHN MORGHEN · CINDY HAMILTON**
FEATURING · TONY KING · WALLACE WILKINSON · RAY WILLIAMS · JOHN GEROSEN · MAY HEATHERLEY
DIRECTED BY **ANTHONY M. DAWSON** PRODUCED BY MAURIZIO and SANDRO AMATI

LA KRISTAL FILM presenta
PORNO HOLOCAUST
con **GEORGE EASTMAN · DIRCE FUNARI · ANNJ GOREN**
MARK SHANON
regia **JOE D'AMATO · COLORE DELLA TELECOLOR**

porn. Zombies and hardcore sex come together for the first time in Aristide Massaccesi's *Erotic Nights of the Living Dead* (1980) and again in *Porno Holocaust* (1981), a poorly directed movie that fails both as a horror film and a porn film. Obviously thieving its title from Ruggero Deodato's seminal *Cannibal Holocaust*, it's about a cannibal/zombie who kills and rapes women with his absolutely huge penis on a remote island. Unlike *Erotic Nights*, *Porno Holocaust* actually features zombie sex, but that's not enough to redeem it from terrible direction and painfully un-erotic sex scenes that are interrupted by bouts of zombie violence that will soften the hardest of horror porn fans. Mario Siciliano's *Erotic Orgasm* (1982) also boasts zombie sex and cannibalism, but both are far too brief to appeal to anyone other than horror porn enthusiasts interested in a limp history lesson.

Even the more conventional living dead tales were often tastelessly sleazy, as Italian zombie films were generally characterized by copious amounts of sex and violence. Umberto Lenzi's *Nightmare City* (1980), Bruno Mattei's *Hell of the Living Dead* (1980), Andrea Bianchi's *Burial Ground* (1981), Pupi Avati's *Revenge of the Dead* (1983), and Lamberto Bava's *Graveyard Disturbance* (1987) are all mediocre to abysmal outings that manage to make quick work of undressing beautiful women in raunchy scenes that often have little or nothing to do with the plot. For example, in an unforgettably bizarre and disturbing scene from *Burial Ground*, a young boy (played by an adult actor with dwarfism) turns into a zombie and takes a bite out of his mother's breast after convincing her to allow him to suckle at it. What else is there to do during a zombie apocalypse but make sexual advances on your mother? This is Eurotrash at its most full-blooded.

TOP LEFT: **John Saxon stars in the cannibal/zombie crossover** *Cannibal Apocalypse* **(1980). Image courtesy Jay Slater.**

TOP RIGHT: **Zombie cannibals in Marino Girolami's** *Zombie Holocaust* **(1980). Image courtesy Jay Slater.**

ABOVE: **Zombies and hardcore porn come together in** *Porno Holocaust* **(1981).**

LEFT: Dirty zombies attack in Bruno Mattei's terrible *Hell of the Living Dead* (1980). Image courtesy Jay Slater.

BOTTOM LEFT TO RIGHT: Andrea Bianchi's tastelessly sleazy *Burial Ground* (1981). Image courtesy Jay Slater.

Jess Franco's *The Devil Hunter* is an expectedly pervy entry in the zombie-cannibal crossover subgenre.

TOP TWO IMAGES: **An entire volleyball team of nude swimmers are molested by underwater zombies in** Jean Rollin's risible *Zombie Lake* **(1981). Images courtesy Jay Slater.**

BOTTOM LEFT: **A toxic spill revives a dead (and often naked) heiress in** The Living Dead Girl **(1982).**

BOTTOM RIGHT: **Bernard Launois's** *Devil Story* **(1985).**

But Italy wasn't the only country getting down with the zombie Eurotrash movement. Sexploitation director Jess Franco dipped his pervy wick in the cannibal subgenre with 1980's *The Devil Hunter* (Spain), which showcases a cannibal chewing off and devouring a woman's labia (!). The sleazy dealings continue as rapist zombies attack women and children in Tomás Aznar's *Further than Fear* (1980, Spain); an entire volleyball team of nude swimmers are molested by underwater zombies in Jean Rollin's *Zombie Lake* (1981, France/Spain); a toxic spill revives a dead (and often naked) heiress in *The Living Dead Girl* (1982, France/Spain); zombie hookers do it for cheap in Ignasi P. Ferré's *Morbus* (1983,

Spain); there's plenty of lesbian sex and cheap zombies on display in Franco's *Mansion of the Living Dead* (1985); and three naked dead girls get down and dirty with a prostitute (and so much more) in Pierre B. Reinhard's *Revenge of the Living Dead Girls* (1987, France). Of course, there are totally mental entries such as Bernard Launois's *Devil Story* (1985, France), and downright soporific outings including Franco's *Oasis of the Zombies* (1981), which, along with *Zombie Lake*, are considered to be among the worst zombie films to come out of the era. This manner of derivative repetition eventually drove the zombie into the ground in Europe.

The 1980s: Undead in the USA

Back on American soil, pioneering films such as Bob Clark's *Black Christmas* (1974), John Carpenter's *Halloween* (1979), and 1980's *Friday the 13th* (itself an imitation of Mario Bava's 1971 thriller *A Bay of Blood*) ushered in a new era of trashy, sex-fueled movies that came to be known as "slasher" films. These movies were sexually tame by comparison to their European progenitors, but they usually featured some manner of masked or disfigured villain pursuing horny teenagers with murder on his or her agenda. While slasher movies were by far the most popular subgenre in the eighties, plenty of studios big and small turned a quick profit with zombie flicks. It would be the most plentiful decade ever for the living dead.

Speaking of *Friday the 13th*, it would be negligent not to point out that the series' main antagonist is, for all intents and purposes, a zombie. In the first film, Jason Voorhees rises out of the lake he had allegedly drowned in years before. He spends the rest of the franchise (which yielded an astonishing eleven sequels) stalking, slashing, killing, and being killed only to rise again—sometimes even from his own grave. He is a seemingly unstoppable supernatural undead mass murderer that, unlike Romero's zombies, cannot be killed by destroying the brain. You can hack him up, slam an axe into his skull, hang him, drown him, drive a machete through his eye, electrocute him, bathe him in toxic waste, and even launch him into space, but he will just . . . keep . . . coming . . . back. For this reason alone, Jason Voorhees is perhaps the most popular and prolific zombie of all time.

It was the era of VHS violence, and it seemed everyone was making shoddy horror films to take advantage of the new video marketplace. Amidst cadres of excruciatingly low-budget, often straight-to-video movies such as *The Children* (1980), *The Alien Dead* (1980), *Battalion of the Living Dead* (1980), *Toxic Zombies* (1980), *Curse of the Screaming Dead* (1982), *I Was a Zombie for the FBI* (1982), *Fear No Evil* (1981), *Kiss Daddy Goodbye* (1981), and *The Aftermath*

(1982), a few gems managed to emerge. John Carpenter's *The Fog* (1980) is a prime example. It centers on a group of long-dead sailors (led by Captain Blake, played by SFX legend Rob Bottin) that rise from their watery graves on the one-hundredth anniversary of their deaths to terrorize the residents of the seaside town of Antonio Bay for stealing their gold. Carpenter insists the supernatural menace in his film is a group of ghosts, but these nautical waterlogged corpses possess a staggering gait and rotten appearance reminiscent of the walking dead.

ABOVE: *Friday the 13th*'s Jason Voorhees is perhaps the most popular and prolific zombie of all time.

They may not be flesh-eaters, but they're definitely zombies—dripping maggots and all. For all its charms, *The Fog* eventually devolves into a siege story à la *Night of the Living Dead* that makes too little use of the creepy zombies. It's a pattern the director would reuse (quite well) in *The Prince of Darkness* (1987) and (not so well) in *Ghosts of Mars* (2001).

Eschewing the fashionable biological disaster explanation for the existence of zombies, a few filmmakers returned to the voodoo themes of the 1940s. Gary Sherman's *Dead and Buried* (1981) is a decidedly Lovecraftian tale about the supernatural goings-on in a spooky New England town named Potter's Bluff. The local sheriff (James Farentino) investigates a series of bizarre accidents that are befalling the townspeople. Stranger still, the victims all return to their daily lives seemingly unharmed after being embalmed. After he discovers occult books in his own wife's drawer, he begins to suspect the local undertaker has been schooling himself in the black arts and controlling the townsfolk. Written by *Alien*'s Dan O'Bannon,

Dead and Buried features outstanding make-up effects by Stan Winston, cringe-worthy death scenes orchestrated by some outrageously cruel zombie townspeople, and an extremely satisfying twist ending that should surprise most viewers.

After shooting *Nightriders* in 1981, Romero returned to the genre that made him a superstar with *Creepshow* (1982), a simple anthology of humorously dark tales penned by famed horror

TOP: **Captain Blake (played by Rob Bottin) leads his crew to their stolen gold in *The Fog*. Image courtesy Michael Felsher.**

ABOVE: **A scorched zombie points the way to the other side in John Carpenter's *Prince of Darkness* (1987).**

novelist Stephen King. Two of the film's five segments were about zombies: "Father's Day" is a dusty little ditty about a family that murders their patriarch to collect inheritances only to get their comeuppance at the hands of their undead daddy at a Father's Day gathering ("I want my cake!"). Like *Tales from the Crypt* (1979) before it, *Creepshow* is inspired by EC Comics' line of horrific morality tales that typically featured wrongdoers punished in the end. This is true for the final segment of the film, "Something to Tide You Over." Leslie Nielsen stars as a paranoid crazy who buries his wife (Gaylen Ross) and her lover (Ted Danson) up to their necks on his secluded beach. They are washed away with the tide but eventually return for revenge as seaweed-caked, gurgling zombies from the depths. With exemplary make-up effects by Tom Savini and oversaturated photography

from cinematographer Michael Gornick, *Creepshow* is a fun, living comic book anthology that has yet to be topped. It's no surprise the film raked in $20 million, way more than its $7 million budget. It was later followed by *Creepshow 2* in 1987, but wasn't directed by Romero and was comprised of three cast-off stories from the first film.

Yes, the living dead were more popular than ever in the eighties. But it wasn't until 1983, when dancing zombies starred in Michael Jackson's music video "Thriller," that the creature experienced true mainstream mega-stardom. The most popular recording artist of the period, Jackson wisely teamed up with one of the most successful horror directors of the period, John Landis (*An American Werewolf in London*), to shoot the most expensive video ever made. Together they created a fourteen-minute

ABOVE LEFT: **Poster for Gary Sherman's *Dead and Buried*.**

ABOVE: **George Romero directs *Creepshow* (1982), based on stories from Stephen King. Two of the anthology's five tales were about zombies.**

musical about a boy (Jackson) and his girl (Ola Ray) who are besieged by a gaggle of ghouls while on a date. Michael is turned and leads the zombies in a twitchy death dance as more of them rise from their tombs and join the freaky festivities. Later he inexplicably becomes a wolfman and, along with the zombies, closes in on his girlfriend who barricades herself in an abandoned farmhouse (in a direct homage to *Night of the Living Dead*).

The video was shot on a budget of $800,000 and featured high-end make-up from effects legend Rick Baker, who won an Academy Award for his work on *An American Werewolf in London*. While sometimes intentionally funny, "Thriller" featured some downright creepy zombie unearthing sequences bolstered by a voiceover from the one and only Vincent Price rapping about "grizzly ghouls from every tomb closing in to seal your doom." "Thriller" remains the most successful music video of its kind, and the dance number has gone on to become a pop-culture phenomenon. Just Google "prisoners Thriller dance" for proof.

By the time "Thriller" emasculated the zombie and brought them moonwalking into living rooms everywhere, the creature already seemed to have its tongue firmly planted in rotting cheek in films like Sam Raimi's outrageously gory *The Evil Dead* (1981). While not a straight-up zombie movie, *The Evil Dead* showcases enough possessed corpses and animated body parts to qualify its inclusion here. Five friends head out to a remote cabin in the woods where they discover an old tape recording containing demonic incantations that unleash forces of evil from another dimension. Much hilarity ensures as sole survivor and hapless hero Ashley J. Williams (Bruce Campbell) reluctantly dismembers his turned friends one by one. Laughter and shock blend perfectly as Raimi assaults the audience with endless barf bag jokes, ingenious camera moves, giggling dead people, and even a rapist tree! Despite the film's comedic intentions (which bordered on slapstick at times), *The Evil Dead* faced major censorship issues both in

North America and abroad. Nevertheless, it become the most successful selling video in 1983 and even spawned a sequel and a musical.

With *Evil Dead II*, Raimi was instructed by producer Dino De Laurentiis to deliver an R-rated film (to the tune of $3.6 million, much more than the $300,000 he had for his first film). To achieve this, the director used copious amounts of blood and goo—in every color save for red. The clever idea being that as long as it ain't red, it ain't blood. *Evil Dead II* is practically a remake of *The Evil Dead*. Ashley J. Williams (again played by Bruce Campbell) finds himself in a strangely familiar cabin dismembering his possessed

TOP: **Zombies are catapulted to mega-stardom in Michael Jackson's 1983 music video "Thriller." Image courtesy Paul Davis.**

ABOVE: **Director George Romero (left) and famed horror-novelist Stephen King (right) collaborate on the darkly humorous anthology film** *Creepshow.*

ABOVE LEFT TO RIGHT:
Theatrical poster for *Evil Dead 2*.

Bruce Campbell (as Ashley J. Williams) battles his own zombified hand and possessed friends in Sam Raimi's *Evil Dead 2* (1987).

Make-up effects artist Greg Nicotero with *Evil Dead 2*'s "Henrietta." Image courtesy Greg Nicotero.

friends and battling demonic "deadites" including his own hand. Here, Raimi blends over-the-top splatter with *Three Stooges*–style comedic violence into a series of gory guffaws that came to be known as "splatstick." This film was such a success it hatched another sequel, *Army of Darkness* (1993)—which was more comedy than horror—making it one of the most popular genre films of all time.

It's into this arena that other humorous zombie films such as *Night of the Comet* (1984) and *The Return of the Living Dead* (1985) arrived. While *Night of the Comet* is a bloodless, sexless, PG-13, teenage programmer, *Return* is a hilarious and horrifying *Night of the Living Dead* spin-off—by far the most successful zombie comedy of the decade. *NotLD* co-writer John Russo (who owned the right to use the phrase "Living Dead" in future film projects) wrote the script for the film, which was at one point going to be directed as a 3D feature by Tobe Hooper (*The Texas Chainsaw Massacre*). After Hooper dropped out to shoot the space-vampire film *Lifeforce*, directing duties fell on co-writer Dan O'Bannon (*Alien*, *Dead and Buried*). He rewrote Russo's script, taking it away

from *NotLD* and further into the realm of black comedy, all while developing the zombie into a new beast.

Trainee Freddy (Thom Matthews) is on his first day at the job with Frank (James Kern) at Uneeda Medical Supply when they stumble upon American military canisters in the basement containing infectious zombies. After explaining that the events in *Night of the Living Dead* actually happened and that these zombies were mistakenly shipped to Uneeda, Frank accidentally cracks open one of the canisters. Both are sprayed with an experimental gas called 245-Trioxin, which knocks them out but reanimates the split dogs and cadavers hanging in the meat locker. They hack up the evidence and take it across the street to a bulgy-eyed embalmer (Don Calfa) who incinerates the body parts, leaking the gas into the outside air where Freddy's punk rock buddies are waiting for him (in the hilariously named Resurrection cemetery). Before you can say, "Do you wanna party?" the dead are rising from their graves, ordering more paramedics on CB radios, and having a flesh fiesta with the unfortunate graveyard loiterers. The gang of

ABOVE: *Evil Dead 2*'s ghoul in the cellar. Image courtesy Greg Nicotero.

living quickly scatter and hole up in both the medical supply warehouse and mortuary as the dead close in. When they contact the number on the side of one of the barrels, the military nukes the entire city, which may or may not spread the contagion to the rest of the nation.

Backed by a punk rock score that included 45 Grave, T.S.O.L., The Damned, and The Cramps, *Return of the Living Dead* was just what the 1980s' teenager ordered—rude, gory, and side-splittingly funny. Add to that inspired acting, a gravestone striptease from scream queen Linnea Quigley, and a slimy, memorable beast called the Tar Man, and O'Bannon had a recipe for success. The film also played with the rules established in George Romero's films. Apart from the fact that O'Bannon's zombies could run as fast as their decomposed legs could take them, *Return of the Living Dead* is also notable for giving the zombie a voice. For the first time, the living dead could talk, hatching the now famous zombie cry for "Braaaaaaaaaaains!" Finally, eating brains specifically was an entirely new twist on the living dead, one that would become a permanent feature of the zombie. Yes, this is the movie

where the zombie developed its taste for human brains. Oh, and they definitely can't be killed by destroying the brain. As Clu Gulager's character notes, "You can chop them up into pieces and the pieces will still come after you."

Hot on the heels of *Return of the Living Dead* was Stuart Gordon's *Re-Animator* (1985). While extremely gruesome, Gordon's gore fest is so playful in its comic absurdity that it's hard to take seriously—especially when the lead spouts lines like, "Who's going to believe a talking head? Get a job in a sideshow." Loosely based on the 1922 story by H. P. Lovecraft, *Re-Animator* centers on the dubious experiments of the mad doctor Herbert West (Jeffrey Combs). West rents the basement of fellow student Dan Cain (Bruce Abbott), who becomes reluctantly embroiled in the kooky scientist's clandestine efforts to reanimate the dead using a glowing green concoction he's invented. A splatter celebration, the film is chock-full of frenzied animated body parts, including an attacking set of intestines (!), and even features a tasteless scene in which a severed head (played by David Gale) attempts to perform cunnilingus on a bound woman

(Barbara Crampton). Shocked by the gleeful violence and perversion on display, the MPAA refused to rate the film, and it was subsequently released to theaters unrated, where it successfully recouped its budget before becoming a home-video hit. The film produced two sequels, *Bride of Re-Animator* (1990) and *Beyond Re-Animator* (2003), both directed by producer Brian Yuzna.

These American zombie films, like many from the decade, abandon any and all possible subtext and give preference to yuk-yuks derived from gross-outs and bodily horror. Good thing Romero was on hand to put the bleakness back in zombie movies with *Day of the Dead* (1985), the third entry in the series that began with *Night of the Living Dead*. It picks up a few years after *Dawn of the Dead*, in a world now entirely consumed by extremely decomposed zombies. A band of scientists and soldiers have holed up in an underground bunker/mine, led by the overly optimistic Sarah (Lori Cardille). Much to the chagrin of the megalomaniacal Captain Rhodes (Joe Pilato), mad doctor Logan (Richard Liberty) has been attempting to domesticate the creatures—sometimes using the remains of Rhodes' men. When the captain finds out, infighting and violence lead to chaos and, ultimately, the dead getting inside.

Audiences used to lighthearted fare like *Back to the Future* and *The Goonies* weren't ready for *Day of the Dead*'s bleak tone and hideous gore. For their part, horror fans weren't either. Though it contains some of the nastiest death scenes ever filmed, *Day* has often been wrongly criticized as being a bit of a bore. This couldn't be further from the truth, because the EC Comics-styled film is depressing as hell, paced quite well, has wildly memorable dialog ("You want me to salute that pile of walking pus? Salute my ass!"), and features ample amounts of blissfully gratuitous gore. The first zombie we see in the film is a nasty bugger missing his lower jaw (dubbed "Dr. Tongue"), another's guts literally spill out of its abdomen as it tries to sit up, and, later in the film, Rhodes is torn asunder

ABOVE: **Dan O'Bannon's hilarious and horrifying** *Night of the Living Dead* **spin-off.**

LEFT: **The zombie developed its taste for human brains in** *Return of the Living Dead*. **Image courtesy Michael Felsher.**

ABOVE: *Re-Animator*'s tagline captures its comical essence: "Herbert West has a good head on his shoulders . . . and another one on his desk."

RIGHT: Jeffrey Combs stars as death-obsessed mad scientist Dr. Herbert West in Stuart Gordon's splatterfest, *Re-Animator* (1985).

FAR RIGHT: Dr. Hill (David Gale), West's adversary.

BOTTOM TWO IMAGES: A couple of Dr. West's victims. Images courtesy Michael Felsher.

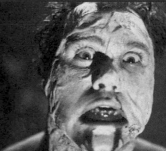

First there was
"NIGHT of the LIVING DEAD"

then
"DAWN of the DEAD"

and now the darkest day of horror the world has ever known

GEORGE A. ROMERO'S

DAY OF THE DEAD™

United Film Distribution Company presents A Laurel Production
George A. Romero's "DAY OF THE DEAD"
Starring Lori Cardille, Terry Alexander, Joe Pilato, Richard Liberty
Production Design Cletus Anderson, Music by John Harrison, Director of Photography Michael Gornick
Makeup Special Effects Tom Savini, Co-Producer David Ball, Executive Producer Salah M. Hassanein
Produced by Richard P. Rubinstein, Written and Directed by George A. Romero
ORIGINAL SOUND TRACK AVAILABLE ON SATURN RECORDS & TAPES

Due to scenes of violence, which may be
considered shocking, no one under 17 admitted.   © MCMLXXXV Dead Films, Inc.

(watch for the whole chicken a zombie pulls out of him!). Beyond that, a soldier's face is literally ripped off, and another's screams increase in pitch as his vocal chords stretch while his head is being pulled from his body—hardly "boring" in any sense. In fact, these are some of the most spectacular gore scenes ever filmed. Tom Savini had his work cut out for him and he delivered.

A pet zombie called "Bub" (played with heart by Sherman Howard), who seems to be able to remember how to use objects from his past, also became a highlight of the film. Bub is Romero's attempt at making us sympathetic to the zombies and not the humans, and it works. While Logan socializes the creature into being more and more human, Rhodes and his men regress and become increasingly barbaric. Civilian pilot John (Terry Alexander) and communications expert McDermott (Jarlath Conroy) have no interest in taking either side and isolate themselves from the group, preferring to live in a converted Winnebago they call "The Ritz." Through the character of John, Romero attempts to return the zombie to its Caribbean roots by offering an explanation for the apocalypse in an impassioned monologue about humanity being punished by the creator: "Maybe He just wanted to show us He was still the boss man. Maybe He figured we was getting too big for our britches trying to figure his shit out."

The film ends with John, McDermott, and Sarah escaping to a Caribbean island where they are evidently waiting for the zombies to rot and disappear—and perhaps take John's advice to start over by making some (interracial) babies. It's the most upbeat ending of the three *Dead* films and was supposed to be the last. *Day* was eventually followed by *Land of the Dead* (2005), *Diary of the Dead* (2007), and, most recently, *Survival of the Dead* (2009). Still, many critics cite *Day* as by far the best of the bunch. We would be inclined to agree.

Okay, so maybe *Day of the Dead* was a little too bleak for audiences during the 1980s, who spent the rest of the decade gobbling up less

serious (and sometimes downright inexcusable) fare like *Gore-Met: Zombie Chef from Hell* (1986), *House* (1986), *The Supernaturals* (1986), *Zombie Nightmare* (1986), *Neon Maniacs* (1986), *Night of the Creeps* (1986), *Redneck Zombies* (1987), *Zombie High* (1987), *The Dead Next Door* (1988), *Dead Heat* (1988), and *Maniac Cop* (1988). But that didn't stop other filmmakers from making the occasional serious zombie picture.

Wes Craven, who previously forayed into the zombie subgenre with *Deadly Friend* (1986), attempted to return the zombie to its voodoo origins in 1987's *The Serpent and the Rainbow*. It stars Bill Pullman and is loosely based on the events in Wade Davis' wildly popular non-fiction book of the same name, which chronicles the (allegedly true) exploits of an ethnobotanist studying a voodoo powder (tetrodotoxin) being used by bokors in Haiti to turn people (specifically a real man named Clairvius Narcisse) into zombies. Upon his arrival in Haiti, Dennis Alan (Pullman) becomes a target for corrupt government officials and evil voodoo priests. The film recounts how evil despots like "Baby Doc"

OPPOSITE: **The zombie apocalypse continues in George Romero's *Day of the Dead* (1985).**

ABOVE CLOCKWISE FROM TOP LEFT: **Dr. Logan attempts to domesticate a pet zombie named Bub (Sherman Howard) with mixed results. Photo courtesy Michael Felsher.**

Tom Savini (pictured) created some of the most spectacularly gory make-up effects ever filmed with *Day of the Dead*.

Duvalier used "zombificiation" to control the populace of Haiti. A slick, modern look at the traditional zombie, *The Serpent and the Rainbow* features some nightmarish scenes of claustrophobia, genital torture, and emotional anguish. And even though the original author of the book hated the final product, horror fans flocked to see it and the other voodoo-themed horror film of the year, *Angel Heart*.

RIGHT: **Director Fred Dekker with *Night of the Creeps'* zombie teenagers. Photo courtesy Michael Felsher.**

MIDDLE: **Robert Z'Dar as a zombie policeman in Bill Lustig's *Maniac Cop* (1988).**

BOTTOM: **Bill Pullman stars as an ethnobotanist studying the existence of a zombie voodoo drug in Haiti in Wes Craven's *The Serpent and the Rainbow* (1987). Photo courtesy Michael Felsher.**

List of the Living Dead

The 1980s was the heyday of the zombie. For further evidence, here's a list of selected titles from that putrid period—some fresh, some downright rotten.

Cannibal Apocalypse (1980) ITALY
Erotic Nights of the Living Dead (1980) ITALY
Devil Hunter (1980) ITALY
The Children (1980) USA
Alien Dead (1980) USA
Faster than Fear (1980) SPAIN
Battalion of the Living Dead (1980) USA
Friday the 13th (1980) USA
City of the Living Dead (1980) ITALY
Encounter of the Spooky Kind (1980) HONG KONG
The Fog (1980) USA
Hell of the Living Dead (1980) ITALY
Nightmare City (1980) ITALY
Toxic Zombies (1980) USA
Zombi Holocaust (1980) ITALY
L'au-delà de la mort (1980) FRANCE
Porno Holocaust (1980) ITALY
The Beyond (1981) ITALY
Burial Ground (1981) ITALY
Oasis of the Zombies (1981) FRANCE/SPAIN
Dawn of the Mummy (1981) ITALY/USA
Fear No Evil (1981) USA
Devil Hunt Danger (1981) USA
The House by the Cemetery (1981) ITALY
Kiss Daddy Goodbye (1981)
Zombie Lake (1981) FRANCE/SPAIN
Erotic Orgasm (1981) ITALY
The Aftermath (1982) USA
Curse of the Screaming Dead (1982) USA
I Was a Zombie for the FBI (1982) USA
The Living Dead Girl (1982) FRANCE/SPAIN
Raw Force (1982) USA/PHILIPPINES
Creepshow (1982) USA
Kung Fu from Beyond the Grave (1982) HONG KONG
Kung Fu Zombie (1982) HONG KONG
Morbus (1983) SPAIN
One Dark Night (1983) USA
Sole Survivor (1983) USA
Revenge of the Dead (1983) ITALY

"Thriller" (1983) USA
Mutant (1984) USA
Night of the Comet (1984) USA
Bloodsuckers from Outer Space (1984) USA
Massacre of the Living Dead (1983) SPAIN
The Midnight Hour (1985) USA
Cemetery of Terror (1985) MEXICO
Day of the Dead (1985) USA
Death Warmed Up (1985) NEW ZEALAND
Hard Rock Zombies (1985) USA
Mr. Vampire (1985) HONG KONG
Re-Animator (1985) USA
The Return of the Living Dead (1985) USA
Devil Story (1985) FRANCE
Amazing Stories "Go to the Head of the Class" (1986) USA
Deadly Friend (1986) USA
Gore-Met Zombie Chef from Hell (1986) USA
House (1986) USA
Raiders of the Living Dead (1986) USA
The Supernaturals (1986) USA
Zombie Brigade (1986) USA
Zombie Nightmare (1986) USA
Zombiethon (1986) USA
Neon Maniacs (1986) USA
Night of the Creeps (1986) USA
Graveyard Disturbance (1987) ITALY
I Was a Teenage Zombie (1987) USA
Redneck Zombies (1987) USA
Revenge of the Living Dead Girls (1987) FRANCE
The Video Dead (1987) USA
Zombie vs. Ninja (1987) HONG KONG
Creepshow 2 (1987) USA
Killing Birds: Uccelli Assassini (1987) ITALY
Prince of Darkness (1987) USA
Rest in Pieces (1987) SPAIN/USA
Zombie Death House (1987) USA
Zombie High (1987) USA
Evil Dead (1981) USA

Night of the Living Babes (1987) USA
Curse of the Blue Lights (1988) USA
The Dead Next Door (1988) USA
FleshEater (1988) USA
Ghost Town (1988) USA
Monsters "My Zombie Lover" (1988) US
Dead Heat (1988) USA
Maniac Cop (1988) USA
Return of the Living Dead Part II (1988) USA
The Serpent and the Rainbow (1988) USA
Zombi 3 (1988) ITALY
Zombie 4: After Death (1988) ITALY
Beverly Hills Body Snatchers (1989) USA
The Chilling (1989) USA
From the Dead of Night (1989) USA
Hellgate (1989) USA
The Laughing Dead (1989)
The Dead Pit (1989) USA
Zombie Rampage (1989) USA
Night Life (1989) USA
Pet Sematary (1989) USA
Tales from the Crypt (1989–1996) USA
The Vineyard (1989) USA
Sheong Hau (1989) THAILAND
Working Stiffs (1989) USA

The 1990s

By the end of the 1980s, the spoof cycle that dominated the decade was grinding to a halt. Too many derivative, Z-rate, no-budget zombie movies flooded the video market, and the public began to lose interest again. As a result, the 1990s saw the release of the fewest zombie movies since the 1940s. The decade was characterized by plenty of sequels—*Maniac Cop 2* (1990), *Bride of Re-Animator* (1990), *Pet Sematary II* (1992), *Maniac Cop 3: Badge of Silence* (1993), *Return of the Living Dead III* (1993)—remakes (*Night of the Living Dead*, 1990), and even a 1998 redux that woefully bastardized *Night of the Living Dead* by adding in fifteen minutes of new footage, written and directed by John Russo.

Mercifully, most of those titles weren't anywhere near as bad as Russo's re-edit of Romero's classic. While we can't in good conscience recommend any of the *Maniac Cop* sequels, *Bride of Re-Animator* isn't half bad if you keep your expectations low. Director Stuart Gordon wasn't interested in making a sequel, so the original producer Brian Yuzna stepped in to helm this even goofier follow-up. Herbert West (Jeffrey Combs) and Dan Cain (Bruce Abbott) are at it again, despite the fact that West died at the end of the first film. This time, the mental medical doctor is sewing body parts together to create grotesque new life forms—including giving Dr. Hill's disembodied head bat wings! Terrible acting, lousy compositing, and bad jokes abound. But what did you expect from a film with a tagline like "Date. Mate. Re-animate"? A romantic subplot? Well, it has that too.

Yuzna also got behind the camera for another living dead romance, the humorless *Return of the Living Dead III*. In this sappy tale of teenage love, army brat Curt (J. Trevor Edmond) revives his recently killed punk rock girlfriend Julie (Mindy Clarke) in his father's military lab—which has been conveniently conducting 245-Trioxin tests for the bio-warfare division. Contradicting the rules of the first two films, Julie doesn't rise as a brains-hungry zombie and at one point even explains how she is able to distract herself from the hunger by giving herself body piercings. The star-crossed lovers are eventually chased into the sewers by both the military and a Latino gang, where not much happens. If you're still living in the nineties and think piercings are cool, it's worth a watch for the body modification makeover scene, but otherwise *Romeo and Juliet* this ain't.

ABOVE LEFT TO RIGHT:
Jeffrey Combs reprises his role as mad doctor Herbert West in Brian Yuzna's *Bride of Re-Animator* **(1990).**

Kathleen Kinmont is Gloria, Dr. West's latest abomination in *Bride of Re-Animator*. **Images courtesy Michael Felsher.**

By far the most controversial zombie movie of the decade was a full-color Hollywood studio remake of *Night of the Living Dead* (1990), produced by John Russo and directed by make-up effects guru Tom Savini (*Dawn of the Dead*, *Day of the Dead*). Columbia Pictures financed the film with the blessing of George Romero, who rewrote the script but nevertheless felt the entire production was motivated by financial concerns (the filmmakers were hoping to recoup financial losses incurred by a missing copyright notice on the 1968 film). Romero was also largely absent for the filming, which was hindered by bickering among the crew and personal problems. The director was never happy with the end product and has since referred to the shoot as "the worst experience of my life."

For what it's worth, Savini's *Night of the Living Dead* is pretty good considering the bad start it had. Admittedly, the gore is surprisingly tame given the pedigree of its director, and the narrative lacks the social commentary of the original. But despite all this, it successfully updates the story, this time with Barbra (Patricia Tallman) as a strong female lead (and only survivor), and adds several in-jokes, clever fake-outs, and twists for the seasoned zombie fan. The film was panned by critics upon its initial release, but now holds a solid 70% rating on film website Rottentomatoes.com.

After a successful collaboration on *Dawn of the Dead*, George Romero and Dario Argento joined forces once more for the anthology film *Two Evil Eyes* (1990), based on two stories from Edgar Allan Poe. Romero tackles a modernized retelling of the zombie-themed "The Facts in the Case of M. Valdemar," while Argento takes on "The Black Cat." It was the second time "Valdemar" had been adapted for screen, having already been told once before by Roger Corman in 1962's *Tales of Terror* starring Vincent Price. This time *Creepshow*'s Adrienne Barbeau plays Jessica Valdemar, the greedy benefactor who will stop at nothing to inherit her ex-husband's fortune—including placing the man in a hypnotic trance in order to embezzle his fortune. When Valdemar

dies in the trance, he is trapped in a world between the living and the dead and telepathically haunts Jessica and her boyfriend from the freezer his body is trapped in.

Some Romero fans were disappointed by the uncharacteristically subdued "Valdemar," which definitely feels padded out (the anthology was originally supposed to be four half-hour segments until John Carpenter and Wes Craven bowed out). With about twenty minutes shaved out of its one-hour running time, this morality tale might hold up against the "Father's Day" segment of *Creepshow* if that story didn't feature Ed Harris doing a ridiculous dance scene.

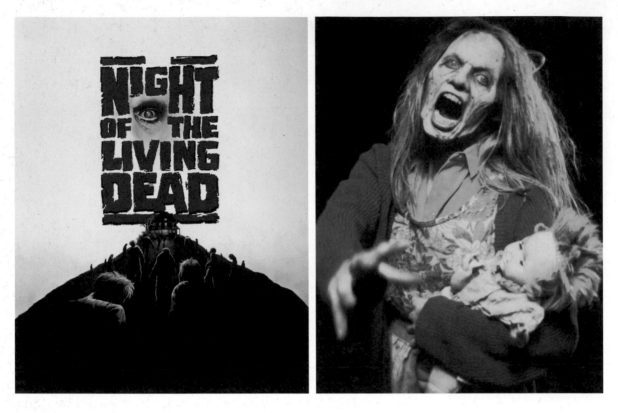

On the indie scene, things were getting much messier. German director Andreas Schnaas thanklessly gave us the gory yet abysmal *Zombie '90: Extreme Pestilence* (1991); Troma delivered the ultra-cheap, ultra-campy *Chopper Chicks in Zombietown* (1991); and Scooter McCrae turned in *Shatter Dead* (1993), a surreal shot-on-video take on the zombie tale (unsurprisingly featuring the Angel of Death as a girl with a strap-on dildo). But no unconventional zombie movie, regardless of budget, could compare to Peter Jackson's outrageously funny and wildly gory splatter opera *Braindead* (1992). By far the best and most memorable zombie film of the decade, New Zealand's *Braindead* (a.k.a. *Dead Alive*) tells the story of Lionel (Timothy Balme), a browbeaten nebbish whose overprotective mother (Elizabeth Moody) turns into a vicious, flesh-hungry demon after she is bitten by a "Sumatran rat monkey" at the zoo. Everyone she attacks—including her nurse and even the family dog—turns into a disgusting zombie. Aided by his new girlfriend Paquita (Diana

Peñalver) and pervy yet resourceful uncle (Ian Watkin), Lionel desperately tries to contain the undead within the family home by turning to household weapons including hedge clippers, a frying pan, a Cuisinart, and even a lawnmower in an infamous scene that went down in history as one of the goriest ever filmed. Equal parts love story and zombie film, *Braindead* is a period piece that, like the director's aptly named *Bad Taste* (1987), must be seen to be believed. Watch out for killer intestines, a zombie baby, and a badass priest who "kicks arse for the lord!"

In stark contrast to the tastelessly gory *Braindead* was more mainstream fare such as Universal's $55 million *Death Becomes Her* (1992) from *Back to the Future* director Robert Zemeckis. It stars Meryl Streep and Goldie Hawn as two beauty-obsessed Beverly Hills socialites who discover the fountain of youth—at the price of their natural lives. They spend the film getting back at one another as Hawn's plastic surgeon fiancé (Bruce Willis) tries to keep the bodies

ABOVE LEFT: **Artwork for Tom Savini's remake of George Romero's** *Night of the Living Dead.*

ABOVE AND OPPOSITE TOP: **Make-up artists John Vulich and Everett Burrell reportedly designed the zombies in** *Night of the Living Dead 1990* **after holocaust victims.**

OPPOSITE BOTTOM: **Barbra (Patricia Tallman) is reinvented as a strong female lead in the remake of** *Night of the Living Dead.*

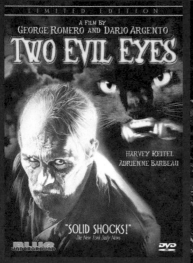

ABOVE: **George Romero and Dario Argento collaborate for the second time for** *Two Evil Eyes* **(1990), based on the works of Edgar Allan Poe.**

TOP MIDDLE: **Lionel Cosgrove (Timothy Balme) is the unwitting nebbish-turned-hero in Peter Jackson's outrageously gory** *Braindead* **(1992).**

TOP RIGHT: **Ian Watkin plays the resourceful, zombie-killing Uncle Les in** *Braindead.*

RIGHT: *Death Becomes Her*: **possibly the most expensive mainstream zombie film ever made.**

they're stuck with forever from literally falling apart. It's pretty tame stuff, but it marks the first time a zombie movie won an Academy Award (for make-up) and probably the only time a zombie movie would earn $150 million at the box office.

The rest of the decade offered a variety of decent time-wasters such *as Uncle Sam* (1997), *Bio-Zombie* (1998), *Plaga Zombie* (1997), *Premutos: Lord of the Living Dead* (1997), and even *Scooby-Doo on Zombie Island* (1998), but none were as inventive and strangely compelling as Italy's *Dellamorte Dellamore* (1994). Director Michele Soavi adapted the tale from a popular novel called *Dylan Dog* (by Tiziano Sclavi), about a cemetery caretaker named Francesco Dellamorte (Rupert Everett) who finds love in the arms of a dead girl. Francesco is an apathetic loner whose job it is to retire people who rise from their graves, which seems to occur exactly seven days after being interred in his cemetery. His best friend is an oafish and decidedly simple creature named Gnaghi (François Hadji-Lazaro), who helps him destroy the undead before they overrun the town. Francesco falls in love with a mourner

at a funeral known only as "She" (Anna Falchi). While consummating their new relationship atop a gravestone, She's husband returns and bites her, turning her into a zombie. This plunges Francesco into a deep depression as he loses his grip on reality. Meanwhile, Gnaghi maintains a love affair with the severed head of the mayor's daughter. Totally unusual and oddly touching, *Dellamorte Dellamore* (a.k.a. *Cemetery Man*) was the last zombie movie to come out of Italy and arguably one of the best.

ABOVE LEFT: **U.S. poster art for Michele Soavi's** *Dellamorte Dellamore* **(a.k.a.** *Cemetery Man***), Italy's best zombie romance.**

ABOVE RIGHT: **Francesco (Rupert Everett) falls for "She" (Anna Falchi) in this oddly touching love story.**

CHAPTER 5

BACK FROM THE DEAD: ZOMBIES IN THE NEW MILLENNIUM

Made in Japan

At the beginning of the twenty-first century, the living dead toiled away in cheaper and crummier features shot on the affordable new medium of digital video in the U.S. Elsewhere, however, it experienced a rebirth. For the first time, Japan was catching on to the zombie craze in a big way. But it wasn't a movie that brought the living dead into the mainstream—it was a video game.

Back in 1996, Capcom producer Shinji Mikami was charged with the task of developing a new horror adventure game for the company's newest console, PlayStation. Modeled after the successful Nintendo haunted house game, *Sweet Home*—itself based on Kiyoshi Kurosawa's film of the same name—*Resident Evil* (released as *Biohazard* in Japan) premiered on PlayStation the same year and garnered rave reviews. It went on to spawn five different versions over the next five years and earn millions for the company.

Mikami looked to both *Night of the Living Dead* and Lucio Fulci's *Zombie* for inspiration for the game: his intention was to make players feel as if they are the main character in a horror movie. In the game, players assume the role of two Special Tactics and Rescue Squad members sent to the fictional town of Racoon City, where the shadowy Umbrella Corporation has released an experimental virus that is turning the residents into flesh-eating zombies. A creepy score, atmospheric locations, and anxiety-inducing tension relieved by sudden zombie attacks bolstered the game's cinematic quality. Because winning relied more on living than collecting points, the game was quickly dubbed by reviewers as "survival horror." Not surprisingly, its popularity resurrected interest in living dead films among teenagers, and a rash of wildly divergent but consistently preposterous zombie outings followed.

Two years after the release of the *Resident Evil* video game, Hong Kong's quirky horror comedy *Bio-Zombie* proved there was money to be made

ABOVE: *Biohazard*, later released in the U.S. as *Resident Evil*, kicked off a resurgence of living dead movies aimed at Japanese gamers.

from Asian zombie video game fans. The film is a witty homage to Romero's *Dawn of the Dead* that takes heavy inspiration from *Resident Evil* and another zombie video game, *House of the Dead*.

While out on an errand, two Bill and Ted-style video store employees (named Woody Invincible and Crazy Bee) accidentally run down a man carrying a soda spiked with a biotoxin, which they feed to the dying man. They take him back to the mall where they work, and all turquoise zombie hell breaks loose. Zombie video games are referenced multiple times throughout, and there's even an onscreen score readout that

tracks health and ammo stats. While it does contain some gore, it's far from scary and has its rotting tongue firmly planted in cheek.

Bio-Zombie paved the way for a series of Japanese zombie films similar in tone, including Atsushi Muroga's *Junk* (2000), Ryūhei Kitamura's *Versus* (2000), Tetsuro Takeuchi's *Wild Zero* (2000), Naoyuki Tomomatsu's *Stacy: Attack of the Schoolgirl Zombies* (2001), Takashi Miike's *The Happiness of the Katakuris* (2001), and Yūdai Yamaguchi's *Battlefield Baseball* (2003).

Most of these films are pretty bombastic and don't take themselves seriously, not the least of which is *Junk*, a forgettable, incoherent jewel-heist flick that blatantly steals from *Aliens*, *The Return of the Living Dead*, *Dawn of the Dead*, *Day of the Dead*, *Re-Animator*, and more. The (distilled) plot: fresh off a robbery, a group of thieves plan to deliver their booty to Yakuza (organized crime members) at a factory that

ABOVE: **Japanese punk band Guitar Wolf star in Tetsuro Takeuchi's** *Wild Zero* **(2000), the wildest rock 'n' roll zombie flick ever made.**

RIGHT: ***Wild Zero* (2000). Poster courtesy Colin Geddes.**

turns out to be an ex-military site, where scientists have been experimenting with a drug that brings the dead back to life. Take a wild guess what happens next. While it's chock-full of splatter, Fulci-esque zombies, and even features a sexy female super zombie who spends most of the film's running time naked, viewers definitely need to switch off their brains to enjoy this . . . er, junk.

Kitamura's *Versus* on the other hand is a far more sophisticated entry that cribs quite successfully from *The Evil Dead* and *The Matrix*. The plot is simple: a group of escaped prisoners, including the sexy Tak Sakaguchi, find themselves double-crossed and trapped in the "Forest of Resurrection" with a bunch of zombies that don't like the Yakuza too much. Much swordplay, arterial spray, and zombie action ensues. While it could benefit from a thirty-minute shave, *Versus* is a highly entertaining and expertly shot martial arts/Yakuza/zombie flick unlike anything you've ever seen.

"Believe in rock 'n' roll!" extol real-life leather-clad Japanese punk band Guitar Wolf, who star in *Wild Zero*, Japan's answer to *Rock 'n' Roll High School*

(but with alien zombies), or *Kiss Meets the Phantom of the Park* . . . with alien zombies. A musical gang of fifties Brooklyn greasers face off against, well, alien zombies, in the wildest Japanese rock 'n' roll zombie flick ever made. Exploding heads, electrified guitar picks, giant fireballs, samurai sword guitars, and pompadours abound in this trashy cult classic. It's totally inept as a horror film but tons of fun. Not to be watched without Googling the "Wild Zero Drinking Game."

The following year, the same production company that brought us *Wild Zero* (Gaga Communications) took silliness to new levels with the formidably low-rent Japanese schoolgirl flick, *Stacy*. Chock-full of groan-inducing zombie film references, including chainsaws named "Bruce Campbell's Right Hand" and the "Romero Repeat Kill Troops," *Stacy* features some of the worst special effects to ever wound retinas on digital video. At the same time, it does take the zombie shtick into a wholly original direction (the disease seems to only afflict teenaged girls) and, as such, is worth checking for a laugh before moving on to Miike's *The Happiness of*

ABOVE LEFT: **Takashi Miike's *Happiness of the Katakuris* can best be described as *The Sound of Music* meets *Night of the Living Dead*.**

ABOVE: **Kenji Sawada, Tetsuro Tanba, and Keiko Matsuzaka are the Katakuris, an unfortunate family whose bed and breakfast guests keep dying and coming back as zombies. Image courtesy Tom Mes at midnighteye.com.**

OPPOSITE TOP: ***Battlefield Baseball* (2003), a goofball zombie sports comedy from *Versus* screenwriter Yūdai Yamaguchi.**

OPPOSITE RIGHT: **Promotional art for *Tokyo Zombie* (2005).**

the Katakuris. This absolutely mental karaoke zombie comedy is a loose remake of Ji-woon Kim's *The Quiet Family* (1998), and has been dubbed *Night of the Living Dead* meets *The Sound of Music* by critics. The story revolves around a family that runs a bed and breakfast in which all of its guests turn up dead, resulting in a zombie problem. It occasionally lapses into monstrous claymation and even features an impromptu musical zombie number. Viewers seeking ultra-violence should look elsewhere. Like the rest of the Japanese zombie films of the period, this one's pure camp.

Last but not least, *Versus* scribe Yūdai Yamaguchi goes goofball with *Battlefield Baseball*, another outrageous horror comedy musical from Japan. *Versus* lead Tak Sakaguchi stars as the thirty-something leader of a high school baseball team that just can't beat the evil (and undead) Goku High team, probably because Goku plays by its own rules, which means killing everyone on the opposing team. Cheap, cartoonish, and overly melodramatic, *Battlefield Baseball* is an absolutely ludicrous adaptation of an equally absurd manga. While these films are definitely enjoyable in their lunatic, screwball way, they couldn't last forever and eventually petered out. The odd Asian zombie film followed, including Thailand's *Sars Wars: Bangkok Zombie* (2004), Hong Kong's *Shaolin vs. Evil Dead* (2004), and *Tokyo Zombie* (2005), but most were far less outrageous than the trashy early zombie comedy classics.

Resident Evil: Western Legacy

Resident Evil was as much of a success in North America as it was in Japan. The game raked in over $600 million worldwide, and it didn't take long before a $35 million American film adaptation was announced. Having previously helmed a successful Japanese television commercial for the video game, George Romero was hired on to direct. But as fate would have it, Romero wasn't the right person for the gig. He was (and still is) most comfortable working outside the studio system, and his initial script was turned down for being "too gory." For a filmmaker who was willing to circumvent the MPAA to stay true to his vision (*Dawn* and *Day of the Dead* were both released unrated rather than with an "X" rating), a studio-imposed R wasn't going to cut it for the seasoned director. Worst of all, Romero didn't even like video games.

He was eventually kicked off the project, much to the dismay of many hardcore horror fans, who chirped like mad all over the internet about the declining state of the genre. For them, *Resident Evil* was already a failure as a horror film even before a single frame had been shot.

RIGHT: **Milla Jovovich stars as Alice, an ass-kicking amnesiac, in Paul W. S. Anderson's *Resident Evil* (2002).**

OPPOSITE: **Poster art for *Resident Evil: Apocalypse* (2004).**

ABOVE: **Now with superhuman strength and psionic abilities, Alice (Milla Jovovich) continues to fight the zombie hordes in the third installment in the film fanchise based on the Capcom survival horror series** *Resident Evil.*

Romero was superseded by George Sluizer (*The Vanishing*), who was quickly fired and replaced by *Mortal Kombat* director Paul W. S. Anderson—a filmmaker and avid gamer who outright insulted the films of Romero and Lucio Fulci while making excuses for why his film was going to lack visceral gore. Despite his claims about making zombie films scary again by removing the senseless gore, the truth was that his intentions were financial and not artistic. This film was aimed at teenaged gamers and it was going to play out that way no matter what. Not surprisingly, when *Resident Evil* was finally released in 2002, it was panned by critics and horror fans alike. But none of that mattered to Capcom, because the franchise-minded *Resident Evil* had already become the most commercially successful zombie film ever made.

Of course, financial success doesn't mean the movie is any good. If the most basic measure of a horror film is its ability to scare an audience,

then *Resident Evil* is a resounding failure. In this formulaic action thriller, Milla Jovovich stars as Alice, an amnesiac who is seized by a group of commandos working for the mysterious Umbrella Corporation and taken to an underground facility called The Hive. The facility is now under control of an AI computer called The Red Queen, which has sealed off the exits after detecting the presence of a contaminant (the experimental T-virus) that has turned the employees into zombies. As the group finds its way to the Queen's chamber, the commandos become fodder for the creatures; Alice fights off skinless dogs and other mutated monsters with her kung fu skills and eventually escapes into a chaos-ravaged Racoon City.

The chief culprit for *Resident Evil*'s failure as a horror film is Anderson's decision to appeal to gamers before moviegoers with his directing style. He employs predictable linear plotting and silly contrivances such as flashing onscreen

maps that are reminiscent of gameplay. Plus, there's a scene that plays out like a gamer facing off against a poorly rendered CGI game "Boss." Sadly, there doesn't seem to be an original moment in the entire movie. Even the film's most tense sequence, in which soldiers are trapped in a corridor of flesh-dicing lasers, is pretty much lifted directly from the 1997 science fiction film *Cube*. The rest plays out like a cutscene from the game, which, incidentally, is far more frightening. Clearly none of this mattered to its teenage audience because the movie's $100 million worldwide box office returns spawned three equally brainless yet successful sequels: *Resident Evil: Apocalypse* (2004), *Resident Evil: Extinction* (2007), and *Resident Evil: Afterlife* (2010), which was shot in 3D using *Avatar*'s Fusion Camera System.

Regardless of what critics and horror fans thought of *Resident Evil*, it managed to drag the zombie into the mainstream, kickstarting

a massive influx of living dead films both big budget and small. It was no surprise when two other video game franchises got the film treatment: Uwe Boll's embarrassing *House of the Dead* (one of the worst zombie films ever made) and the only slightly better *Doom* (2005). Of course, there were always the Camcorder Coppolas and indie filmmakers, making crummy direct-to-video cheapies such as *The Dead Hate the Living!* (2000), *Children of the Living Dead* (2001), and super-splatterfests such as Argentina's *Plaga zombie: Zona mutante* (2001) and Spain's *Mucha Sangre* (2002). That hadn't changed. But as Danny Boyle's *28 Days Later* (2002) proved, shot-on-video zombie films could very much enjoy healthy box office returns internationally—if they were done right.

ABOVE LEFT: **Resident Evil** inspired the release of other science fiction/horror movies based on popular video games, including 2005's *Doom*. Said film critic Roger Ebert, "*Doom* is like some kid came over and is using your computer and won't let you play."

ABOVE: **A zombie with a serious case of periodontitis in Dave Parker's low-budget zombie film *The Dead Hate the Living!* (2000).**

28 Days Later

Shot for $8 million, *28 Days Later* presents a large-scale apocalyptic vision of a plague-ravaged London. Bike courier Jim (Cillian Murphy) wakes up from a coma in a deserted hospital twenty-eight days after an extremely virulent manmade virus called "Rage" has begun to turn citizens into red-eyed, maniacal killers. After narrowly avoiding being killed by a few of "the infected," Jim encounters a handful of survivors, and they leave the capital in search of safety. They eventually run into a group of abusive *Day of the Dead*–inspired soldiers holed up in a military fortress in Manchester. As in Romero's third *Dead* film, the power hungry, rapist soldiers (who even have a pet zombie reminiscent of *Day*'s "Bub") pose more of a threat to the survivors than the infected, and the group must fight their way out of captivity.

Yes, *28 Days Later* borrows heavily from *Day of the Dead*, but it also deliberately distances itself from Romero's zombie paradigms. In fact, the director even stated he didn't see his film as part of the zombie lineage at all. True enough, Boyle's zombies aren't really zombies; they're living people turned violent murderers (a conceit previously employed in films such as 1980's *Cannibal Apocalypse* and Romero's *The Crazies*). They also turn just a few seconds after contact with any infected bodily fluid. Finally—and most importantly—they're capable of running, a characteristic totally new to the zombie subgenre.

Boyle's semantic hang-ups aside, *28 Days Later* is without a doubt a contemporary zombie movie that plays out like Richard Matheson's *I Am Legend* meets Romero's *The Crazies* with "running zombies." In this way, the film succeeds where countless others have not: it made the zombie scary again simply by increasing its speed. The movie was shot with two different endings for the British and American film markets. The U.S. version is considerably darker and generally preferred by horror fans. The film's success ($83 million worldwide at the box office) led to a high-action sequel called *28 Weeks Later* in 2007.

ABOVE: **Danny Boyle's shot-on-video *28 Days Later* (2002) introduced the concept of the "running zombie" into the consciousness of horror fans.**

A human-engineered virus called "Rage" turns people into red-eyed, maniacal killers in *28 Weeks Later* (2007), the high-action sequel to Danny Boyle's *28 Days Later*.

Re-Animation of a Genre

Meanwhile, in America, the low-budget zombie film continued its now consistent tradition of combining humor with horror. Thirteen years after *Bride of Re-Animator*, Brian Yuzna was plumbing what was left of the franchise with *Beyond Re-Animator* (2003). This time Dr. West (again played by Jeffrey Combs) figures out how to inject personalities into his zombies—all while incarcerated in a penitentiary. Apart from a hilarious stop-motion rat versus penis showdown that plays out after the credits roll, there's not much new here to recommend.

In Australia, talented twin brothers Peter and Michael Spierig paid homage to the alien-zombie drive-in movie with *Undead* (2003), an ambitious horror comedy in the vein of Peter Jackson's early work. It's chock-full of nods to *Braindead*, *The Evil Dead*, Romero's *Dead* films, and *Close Encounters of the Third Kind*, and features some truly inspiring gore (from one-man make-up-effects wiz Steve Boyle) and effects sequences created on a PC using After Effects! The Spierigs have since taken on the vampire subgenre with the futuristic bloodsucker vehicle *Daybreakers* (2010). Other lighthearted but gore-soaked zombie efforts followed, including Elza Kephart's *Graveyard Alive: A Zombie Nurse in Love* (2003), Miguel Ángel Lamata's *Una de zombis* (2003), Matthew Leutwyler's *Dead & Breakfast* (2004), David Gebroe's *Zombie Honeymoon* (2004), Germany's *Night of the Living Dorks* (2004), and, of course, the hugely successful *Shaun of the Dead* (2004).

This British zom-rom-com from *Spaced* director (and self-professed *Resident Evil* game junkie) Edgar Wright virtually came out of nowhere and suckerpunched viewers with a blend of extremely clever satire and moments of genuine creepiness. It's a love letter to *Dawn of the Dead* that won over both horror fans and casual viewers. In the film, a zombie plague hits London just as Foree Electric (get it?) employee Shaun (Simon Pegg) gets dumped by his girlfriend. He and his unemployed fat slob of a best friend Nick (Nick Frost) try to make things right as they lead a group of Shaun's friends and family through the zombie carnage to the proposed safety of the local pub, where they stand off against the ghouls using their video game skills ("Reload! Top left! Nice shot!"). *Shaun* was a smash hit at sneak screenings including San Diego Comic-Con, where this writer saw it with a very impressed George Romero, Ken Foree (*Dawn of the Dead*),

ABOVE LEFT TO RIGHT:
Twin brothers Peter and Michael Spierig pay homage to alien-zombie drive-in movie with *Undead* (2003), an ambitious Australian horror comedy in the vein of Peter Jackson's *Braindead*.

OPPOSITE, CLOCKWISE FROM TOP:
***Spaced* director Edgar Wright teams up once again with actors Simon Pegg and Nick Frost.**

The *Shaun of the Dead* director, Edgar Wright, with one of the hero zombies in his film.

***Shaun of the Dead*: 2004's breakout British zom-rom-com won over audiences with its clever blend of satire and horror.**

and Greg Nicotero (*Day of the Dead*) in attendance. Not only was it an instant classic, it was further evidence of *Resident Evil*'s influence on the zombie renaissance.

In 2004, several less intentionally comedic living dead efforts were released, such as Ireland's bovine-themed *Dead Meat* (2004), France's touching *Les revenants* (2004), and even an absolutely shameful and despicable in-name-only sequel to *Day of the Dead* from directors Ana Clavell and James Glenn Dudelson. But without a doubt,

the most high profile zombie film of the year was a big-budget studio remake of *Dawn of the Dead*.

It was with dollar signs in its eyes that Universal—the studio that brought us some very famous monsters—bankrolled a $28 million redux of George Romero's 1978 classic *Dawn of the Dead* (without the blessing of the filmmaker). Thanks to the *Resident Evil* movie, the zombie was more profitable than it had ever been, so the studio saw fit to hire music video director Zack Snyder to helm the picture (rewritten by

Troma alumnus James Gunn) and aim it at a younger, MTV-loving audience.

In this unnecessary remake, a group of survivors—including a nurse (Sarah Polley), an ex-marine cop (Ving Rhames), an electronics salesman (Jake Weber), a street thug (Mekhi Phifer), his pregnant wife (Inna Korobkina), a couple of redneck security guards, and a bunch of other underdeveloped characters—hole up in an abandoned Milwaukee shopping mall after a mysterious virus (transmitted via bite) has turned humans into sprinting, psychotic, flesh-eating cannibals. Besides the money-bearing title, that's about all this movie has in common with its namesake. Not surprising given that Snyder had never even seen any of the *Dead* films prior to taking on the gig. In the end, the survivors attempt to flee the mainland in search of safety by boat. A note to the producers who tacked on the painfully forced ending: there are no "uninhabited islands to live on" in Lake Michigan.

The film was a surprise hit and still manages to be the subject of ongoing debate among horror fans because of its "running zombies," surely inspired by *28 Days Later*. The film also suffers from an overabundance of pointless characters (including a ridiculous zombie baby); disorienting fast editing; tension-spoiling cameos (from Tom Savini, Ken Foree, and Scott Reiniger); a lack of genuinely frightening scenarios, meaningful subtext, or character development; and general disrespect for the source material. While the first ten minutes of the film will surely not disappoint action fans (it captures instant social collapse quite effectively), the remainder has been the target of heavy criticism from genre purists. I myself was a zombie in the film and can't in good conscience recommend it over the original. No self-respecting horror critic would. But casual horror fans and Johnny-come-latelies are guaranteed to love it.

ABOVE LEFT: **In 2004, Universal bankrolled a $28 million redux of George Romero's 1978 classic** *Dawn of the Dead*, **this time featuring controversial running zombies.**

ABOVE: **Running zombies, the subject of ongoing debate among horror fans, in the 2004 remake of** *Dawn of the Dead.*

OPPOSITE: **Poster art for the 2004 remake of Romero's** *Dawn of the Dead.*

Re-Making a Genre

Dawn of the Dead was among the first few films in a new trend of mostly uninspired big-budget Hollywood remakes of horror films from the seventies and eighties, including *The Texas Chainsaw Massacre*, *The Amityville Horror*, *The Hills Have Eyes*, *Black Christmas*, *Halloween*, *The Last House on the Left*, *Friday the 13th*, and *A Nightmare on Elm Street*.

Even more shameful than the pointless remakes were the in-name-only sequels to Dan O'Bannon's 1985 punk-rock zombie opus, *The Return of the Living Dead*. *Return of the Living Dead: Necropolis* and *Return of the Living Dead 5: Rave to the Grave*—released back-to-back on the Sci-Fi Channel in 2005 alongside the equally unforgivable *House of the Dead 2: Dead Aim*—are among the worst zombie films ever made, just one nimble step above *Day of the Dead 2: Contagium*. Both are to be avoided like, ahem, the plague.

Tobe Hooper's *Mortuary* was also released in 2005, a surprisingly incompetent entry from the once-prominent genre director. Zombie fans would fare slightly better tuning in to the director's zombie-themed episode of television's *Masters of Horror* ("Dance of the Dead") from the same year. More notable living dead entries from that series include Joe Dante's poignant "Homecoming" and John McNaughton's adaptation of Clive Barker's "Haeckel's Tale." That episode was originally set to be directed

by George Romero, who was busy making his first zombie feature in twenty years.

Romero had in fact been working at trying to get another original zombie film off the ground since 2000 but it wasn't until the *Resident Evil* films and the remake of *Dawn of the Dead* turned huge profits that Universal Studios finally kicked him $17 million to make *Land of the Dead* (previously titled *Twilight of the Dead* and *Dead Reckoning*). It picks up sometime after *Day of the Dead*; zombies have overrun the globe, and a group of survivors have managed to escape the hordes in a fortified urban compound presided over by a rich opportunist dictator named Kaufman (Dennis Hopper). He and his cronies have taken up residence in a luxury sky rise called Fiddler's Green, while the less fortunate survivors eke out an existence on the streets within the compound.

Kaufman takes advantage of the populace that keeps him eating fine foods and smoking cigars until a disgruntled scavenger named Cholo (John Leguizamo), who was denied residence in Fiddler's Green because of his race, commandeers a battle truck called the Dead Reckoning and threatens to destroy the compound unless his demands are met. In an overt commentary on George W. Bush's War on Terror, Kaufman "refuses to negotiate with terrorists" and sends Cholo's fellow food foragers Riley (Simon Baker) and Charlie (Robert Joy) out to retrieve the vehicle and stop him from leading the zombies into Fiddler's Green.

Meanwhile, the dead are slowly mobilizing with weapons and heading toward the compound. It's an undead revolution led by a zombie known as Big Daddy (Eugene Clark, in a continuation of *Day of the Dead*'s Bub), who has retained the ability to remember and learn tasks. He is oddly outraged and hurt when he sees his kind destroyed and has had enough. Here, Romero explicitly asks us to sympathize with the zombies—perhaps too much. Big Daddy's battle cries are more than a little cheesy as he leads his army toward Fiddler's Green. Eventually the zombies invade, destroy the class system established by Kaufman (along with the dictator himself), and move on, prompting a rather goofy line of dialog from Riley about how the zombies are "like us—just looking for a place to go."

Packed with nasty zombies and outrageous gore sequences from Greg Nicotero, *Land of the Dead* is the most action-oriented zombie film in Romero's canon. Though it grossed over $40 million and garnered generally positive reviews, there is definitely an overabundance of unnecessary characters here, and some of the zombies are downright cheesy (baseball zombie and chef zombie come to mind), but overall it's a decent, if flawed, entry in the *Dead* series.

And the zombie invasion continued with plenty of indie movies hitting theaters and DVD players in 2006. Some were okay (*Fido*), some were not-so-great (*The Zombie Diaries*), but none could be worse than *Night of the Living Dead 3D* (2006), the pathetic, migraine-inducing remake of

TOP: **George Romero returned to the subgenre that made him legend after a twenty-year absence with 2005's *Land of the Dead*.**

ABOVE: **In a continuation of the theme Romero started in *Day of the Dead*, *Land*'s zombies are capable of learning and eventually mount an attack on Fiddler's Green. Here, they are distracted by fireworks.**

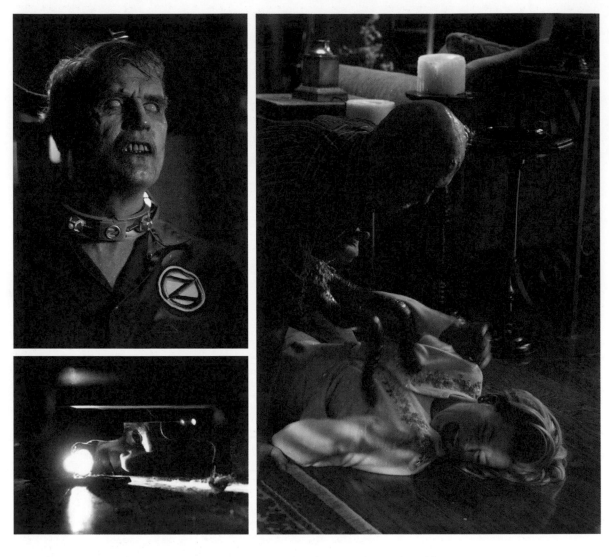

CLOCKWISE FROM TOP LEFT:
Comedian Billy Connolly stars as the titular *Fido* in the 2005 horror-lite comedy from Canadian director Andrew Currie.

Alien slugs turn the simple townsfolk of Wheelsy into zombies in James Gunn's underrated horror comedy, *Slither* (2006).

A virus spreads among the New York population, while a group of tenants trapped in a Manhattan apartment block must fight for survival in 2006's *Mulberry Street*.

Romero's seminal zombie film. When Troma's *Poultrygeist: Night of the Chicken Dead* (2006) does significantly better at the box office, you know you've made a bad zombie movie.

In Canada, director Andrew Currie domesticated the zombie with his extremely horror-lite comedy *Fido* (2006). In the film, a corporation called Zomcon has figured out how to control zombies via an electronic collar and subs them out to local residents for various household chores. Scottish comedian Billy Connolly plays Fido, the titular zombie of the film, which can be best described as *Lassie* meets *Day of the Dead*.

Fido is cute, but it's a one-trick pony that oddly appeals to housewives as well as horror fans. For those seeking more R-rated zom-com action, *Dawn of the Dead* remake scribe James Gunn thankfully stepped behind the camera with his hilarious $15 million B-movie send up, *Slither* (2006). This often misunderstood and overlooked paean to *Night of the Creeps* is a shlocky blend of absurdity and body horror, which failed to recoup its budget at the box office but is assuredly worth seeking out on DVD. Also ripe for DVD pickings is *Mulberry Street* (2006), a zombie/nature-run-amok crossover film about a group of everyday people trapped in a New York

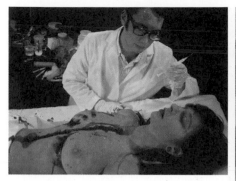

THEY'LL DANCE FOR A FEE, BUT DEVOUR YOU FOR FREE!

sonypictures.com/zombiestrippers

tenement as the populace becomes infected with a virus that transforms people into vicious, mutated rat people.

Deep underground, beneath the direct-to-video cheapies, a bizarre subgenre was forming: zombie porn. Beginning with *Re-Penetrator* (2004) and *The Stink of Flesh* (2005), zombies were beginning to get scared stiff and, by 2007, some had developed a serious case of rigor mortis in just one particular organ: the penis. Rob Rotten's *Porn of the Dead* (2007) pushed the limits of bad taste with its mixture of hardcore porn and hardcore horror. It was followed by other XXX titles including *Zombie Nation* (2008), *Night of the Giving Head* (2008), and Burningangel.com's *Dong of the Dead* (2009). While these titles are admittedly amusing in a goofy way, it's hard to take them seriously as either porn or horror films. Like a speedball, zombie porn is designed to excite and bring you down all at once— that is, unless you're actually turned on by watching dicks being chewed off.

Bruce La Bruce's gay zombie porn film *Otto; or, Up with Dead People* (2008) makes a decent attempt at working hardcore porn into a documentary-style film, but the balance never seems to be quite right. For some, there's not enough porn and for others there's not enough horror. Still, that hasn't stopped La Bruce from shooting another gay zombie porn film, tentatively titled *LA Zombie*.

If undead hardcore gay sex isn't your thing, there are plenty of naked dead dames in *Zombie*

Strippers (2008, featuring porn star Jenna Jameson) and *Strippers vs. Zombies* (2008), but you'd have to be pretty desperate for boob shots to sit through either of them. And let's face it, it's not like you can't see more of Jameson in dozens of other films dedicated to showcasing her assets.

TOP LEFT: **Zombies go hardcore (again) in the 2004 *Re-Animator* spoof, *Re-Penetrator*. Image courtesy Burningangel.com.**

ABOVE: **XXX-star Jenna Jameson guest stars in *Zombie Strippers* (2008) alongside Robert (Freddy Krueger) Englund.**

Reaching the End of the Millennium Decade

As the end of the decade closed in, the zombie continued its relentless invasion on the remake front. Both *Invasion of the Body Snatchers* and *I Am Legend* were remade (poorly) for a third time in 2007, and Steve Miner (*Friday the 13th Part 2* and *III*) wasted his time on an embarrassing redux of *Day of the Dead* (2008) that only served to piss people off. Breck Eisner also stripped *The Crazies* of its social commentary in 2010 and delivered a painfully dull run-and-hide movie that masquerades as a horror film through the use of loud noises.

Almost to make up for these travesties, Robert Rodriguez turned in a refreshingly fun living-dead vehicle with *Grindhouse: Planet Terror* (2007), a film that blends action, horror, comedy, and sci-fi into one complete drive-in experience.

There were also a few laughs to be had with *Flight of the Living Dead: Outbreak on a Plane* (2007), the Western zom-com *Undead or Alive* (2007), the trashy *Trailer Park of Terror* (2007), Glenn McQuaid's quirky period piece *I Sell the Dead* (2008), the zombie buddy picture *The Revenant* (2009), and Jake West's all-female zombie film *Doghouse* (2009). Then there was *Dead Snow* (2009), a Norwegian Nazi zombie comedy and love letter to Sam Raimi's *The Evil Dead*. The film, which is packed with silly gore gags and goofy horror references, was a surprise hit on the festival circuit, earning it a reputation as the "most fun zombie movie of the decade." But *Dead Snow* would lose that title just a few months later when *Zombieland* premiered to major box office and critical success. It features one of the best opening title sequences ever captured on film and a hilarious celebrity cameo that overshadow the movie's few flaws. *Zombieland* reportedly grossed more than $60.8 million in seventeen days, making it the top-grossing zombie film to date. It was around this time that Pakistan released its first zombie movie. Omar Khan's *Hell's Ground* (from a screenplay by Mondo Macabro imprint topper Pete Tombs)

RIGHT: ***Planet Terror*: A deadly biochemical agent known as DC2 turns residents of a small town into bloodthirsty psychopaths in Robert Rodriguez's wildly entertaining tribute to the zombie film genre.**

BELOW: ***Doghouse*: Women become infected with a toxin that turns them into man-hating cannibals in this British zombie comedy from Jake West.**

represents the melding of Lollywood and gritty seventies horror into a mélange of spectacularly gory nonsense that gives *Cannibal Holocaust* a run for its money. *Splinter*, from 2008, and 2009's *Pontypool* offered unique twists on the zombie subgenre. The latter is a high-brow concept (based on a book by Tony Burgess) about a zombie plague that's transmitted through the English language, while the other deals with a fungal parasite with the power to turn its victims into deadly hosts that try to consume survivors barricaded in a gas station. The Don of the Dead, George Romero, also turned in two more zombie films slightly outside of the "Dead" universe, despite their titles. *Diary of the Dead* (2007)

employs a tired, *Blair Witch*-style documentary esthetic as it tells the story of a group of film students trying to cope with the early days of the outbreak while making a horror movie. It's a poorly executed conceit that's put to better use in the genuinely creepy Spanish zombie film *[REC]* (2007), remade the following year in the U.S. as *Quarantine*. While on a ride-along with the local fire department, a television crew is sent into an apartment building to save a trapped old lady. Soon they are locked in with the tenants, some of whom are becoming increasingly violent. An ambiguous ending that hints at a unique religious explanation for the infection is further explored in the equally spine-

TOP LEFT: **The Rotten Reich return to terrorize a group of young vacationers in the Norwegian Nazi zombie comedy, *Dead Snow* (2009).**

TOP RIGHT: **A startled lead in *Zibahkhana* (a.k.a. *Hell's Ground*, 2007), Pakistan's first zombie film.**

ABOVE LEFT AND MIDDLE: **Survivors of a post-zombie apocalypse take a hilarious road trip in *Zombieland*, a hugely successful zombie comedy.**

ABOVE: **A zombie plague is transmitted via the English language in Bruce McDonald's *Pontypool* (2009).**

chilling sequel, *[REC] 2* (2009), from directors Jaume Balagueró and Paco Plaza.

Romero's most recent zombie outing, 2010's *Survival of the Dead*, is unfortunately his weakest. Set on an island somewhere off the coast of North America, *Survival* is a Western-styled piece revolving around two feuding families trying to stay alive and find a cure for the epidemic that's plaguing their peaceful home. Poorly executed CGI gore, bad fake Irish accents, and the introduction of a group of outsiders we care nothing about mire this otherwise fair attempt at reminding us once again that, in times of crisis, we are much worse to each other than the zombies could ever be.

At time of writing, the zombie movie renaissance that began with *Resident Evil* shows no signs of slowing down. Writer Paul W. S. Anderson returned to the director's chair for the fourth installment in the franchise, *Resident Evil: Afterlife*, which Anderson said will kick off a new 3D trilogy. There are plenty more awaiting release, including a new African zombie film called *The Dead* (co-directed by brothers Howard J. Ford and Jonathan Ford), the action-oriented French zombie gangster movie *The Horde* (from directors Yannick Dahan and Benjamin Rocher), as well as a low-budget Canadian effort called *Autumn*. Wesley Snipes stars as a cursed gunman whose victims come back from the dead in *Gallowwalker*, a film that took a hiatus from production as its star faced tax evasion charges in the U.S., and Danny Dyer stars in the *28 Days Later* clone *Devil's Playground*. Both were scheduled for release in 2010.

And there are dozens more in development. The Zack Snyder-produced *Army of the Dead* has been temporarily put on the back burner while its director, Matthijs van Heijningen Jr., shoots the prequel to John Carpenter's *The Thing*. It focuses on a father who tries to keep himself and his daughter alive in a zombie-infested Las Vegas. On the literary front, Max Brooks' best-selling novel *World War Z* has been optioned for feature film adaptation in 2012, along with S. G.

Browne's black comedy *Breathers: A Zombie's Lament*. Grahame-Smith's mash-up *Pride and Prejudice and Zombies* is getting the video game and feature film treatment in 2011. Elsewhere, producers are looking to comic books for new zombie film inspiration: Robert Kirkman's popular graphic novel series *The Walking Dead* made its debut as a television series in 2010, Steve Niles' zombie-themed comic *Wake the Dead* is in the hands of director Jay Russell, and *Watchmen* scribe David Hayter is set to adapt Vincent Locke's classic comic *Deadworld* into a zombie feature franchise. The Italian horror comic *Dylan Dog*, which served as the inspiration for *Dellamorte Dellamore* (a.k.a. *Cemetery Man*, 1994), has been adapted by Canadian filmmaker Kevin Munroe for film as *Dead of Night*, set for release in 2011.

But that's not all. Every day new titles pop up on the internet: Valeri Milev's *Re-Kill*, Ben Hibon's animated film *A.D.*, Shaun Robert Smith's Nazi zombie movie *The 4th Reich*, Patrick Lussier's *Condition Dead 3D*, and Julian Richards' *Dead By Dawn* are all slated for release between 2011–2012, followed by sequels to *Zombieland*, *Quarantine*, and even a proposed remake of Jacques Tourneur's *I Walked With a Zombie*— from the producers of the *Saw* franchise.

And they just keep coming and coming in a relentless onslaught. For the time being, there seems to be no end in sight, proving you just can't keep a good zombie down.

OPPOSITE, FROM TOP: ***Diary of the Dead***: **A crew making a horror film capture the zombie apocalypse in the fourth film in Romero's *Dead* series; Poster art for Romero's *Survival of the Dead*.**

TOP: **The documentary aesthetic is put to good use in Spain's *[REC]* (2007), remade the following year as *Quarantine*.**

MIDDLE AND BOTTOM: **The equally spooky sequel *[REC] 2* (2009) takes the zombie film in a unique direction; Art from nazi-zombie film *The 4th Reich*.**

CHAPTER 6

ZOMBIES
GO
MULTIMEDIA

Nineties Literature

Zombies may have shuffled into pop-culture consciousness through the medium of film, but their popularity with the masses proved so powerful that they couldn't remain confined to celluloid alone. Although the living dead did make some appearances in earlier literature—most notably in Shelley's *Frankenstein* and the travel writings of Lafcadio Hearn—it wasn't until horror authors John Skipp and Craig Spector brought out *Book of the Dead* that zombie literature became a recognized modern horror subgenre in its own right, paving the way for scores of imitators.

Published in 1989, *Book of the Dead* revolves around the premise that a zombie apocalypse is in the making; the short stories chronicle various reactions and struggles by the common people on the ground. With an appropriate foreword by George Romero—as the book largely takes place in the world he imagined in *Night of the Living Dead*—and contributions from such horror masters as Stephen King, Ramsey Campbell, and Douglas E. Winter, *Book of the Dead* proved a hit with horror fans and is often considered the prototype to today's glut of zombie lore. A sequel, *Still Dead: Book of the Dead 2*, was published three years later and features a foreword by Romero's go-to gore man Tom Savini. Perhaps more importantly, it contains stories not only by the old guard of horror—including K. W. Jeter and Mort Castle, as well as another entry from Winter—but also brings a more modern, feminine approach to the genre by showcasing the efforts of Nancy A. Collins, Elizabeth Massie, and Poppy Z. Brite. Both books are well worth a read for their entertainment value as well as their significance to the subgenre, but the sequel is arguably the more accomplished and provides a larger measure of diversity in its authors.

Further undead offerings from the nineties comprise a fairly lame bunch; *The Mammoth Book of Zombies* (1993), edited by Stephen Jones, is probably the most high-profile anthology aimed at adult readers to come out of the

decade, if not entirely original or stand-out. Young adults and children, on the other hand, had quite a few titles to choose from—mostly with a humorous bent—including 152-page *Steven the Zombie* from teenage fiction's most revered and reviled series of all time, *Sweet Valley High/Sweet Valley Twins*. One could be forgiven for thinking that anything appearing in a *Sweet Valley* book was over before it even began, but zombies are nothing if not resilient,

LEFT: **Regarded as the first proper book of zombie literature, *Book of the Dead* spawned a second volume and scores of imitators.**

OPPOSITE: **Stephen Jones has edited several anthologies, both on zombies and horror in general, including the annual *Best New Horror* collections.**

THE MAMMOTH BOOK OF

Zombies

Edited by
Stephen Jones

Clive Barker
Robert Bloch
Ramsey Campbell
Hugh B. Cave
Dennis Etchison
Christopher Fowler
M. R. James
Joe R. Lansdale
H. P. Lovecraft
Brian Lumley
Graham Masterton
Karl Edward Wagner
and many more . . .

By the mid-nineties, even the Wakefield twins were messing with voodoo, rendering the religion terminally uncool.

Max Brooks' highly entertaining breakthrough zombie book.

The graphic novel version is an adaptation of the list of attacks at the end of *The Zombie Survival Guide*, rather than the whole book, but a fun read nonetheless.

and they managed to survive association with the Wakefield twins to find a literary renaissance in the new millennium.

Once Y2K turned out to be a complete waste of decent panic, many horror fiction writers turned their attention to another potential apocalypse, one born most often of pestilence or man-made disaster and christened by the walking dead.

While adaptations of the popular and beloved *Resident Evil* series of video games had been surfacing since the late nineties, it wasn't until the millennium ticked over that zombie books became a serious pursuit for adult fiction writers. Though not published until 2003, the impact of Max Brooks' deft nonfiction-style manual *The Zombie Survival Guide* on the world of horror literature cannot be underestimated. As Mel Brooks' son and a former writer for *Saturday Night Live*, Brooks (mostly) left humor behind in tackling the logistics of preparing for and surviving a zombie outbreak. The *Zombie Survival Guide*'s matter-of-fact, academic tone—combined with the fact that Brooks has obviously spent way too much time thinking seriously about what he would do in the event of a zombie apocalypse—make it a well-researched and realistic-seeming guide to survival in "an undead world," without being overly depressing. If you've ever wondered whether a handgun or a machete provides the surest protection against the living dead in a close-combat scenario (and really, who hasn't?), Brooks' considered, deadpan arguments are a necessary read.

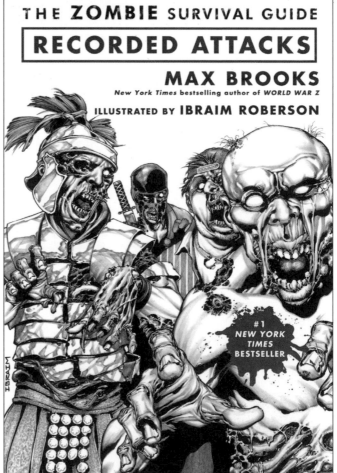

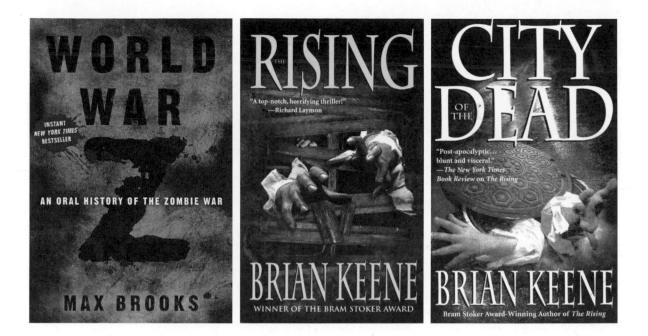

Perhaps most interesting, however, is the list of "Documented Encounters" at the back of the book. Largely based on actual historical events and unsolved mysteries—including the disappearance of the Roanoke, Virginia, colonists—Brooks posits zombie infection as the true reason for these events, citing Hierakonpolis, Egypt, as the site of the first zombie outbreak on Earth in 3,000 BC (because, according to Brooks, the possible outbreak in 60,000 BC Africa is still in dispute). This short but fascinating list seems to form the inspiration for Brooks' next zombie-themed book, *World War Z: An Oral History of the Zombie War* (2006), in that it concentrates more on the human element of the zombie apocalypse and brings the "What if?" scenario into full play.

Taking place ten years after a fictional worldwide zombie outbreak, *World War Z* is set up as a series of short first-person narratives gathered by a roving member of the United Nations Postwar Commission. Brooks' zombies pay homage to Romero: they are properly dead (reanimated by the virus Solanum), mindless, slow moving, and flesh-eating. What sets *World War Z* apart from previous zombie books and films is its totality;

the scale of the zombie outbreak is global, overwhelming the human populace to near extinction. The sheer imagined scale of the apocalypse is terrifying, and while that terror and destruction forms a common narrative thread throughout the stories, Brooks' emphasis on individual suffering and experience gives the book a powerful human element. While the enemy may be complete fiction, the responses to it—from the most powerful government on the planet down to the lowliest dog trainer—seem all too real. And when that reality includes firebombing mixed zombie and human crowds, or eating a neighbor to prevent starvation, the knowledge that "zombie apocalypse" is just a metaphor for any wide-scale disaster very much within the realm of possibility today is a horrifying thought indeed.

Often cited as being at least partly responsible for the rise in twenty-first-century zombie fiction, horror author Brian Keene's first novel, *The Rising* (2003), features a different kettle of zombies from Brooks' Romero-inspired walking dead altogether. Keene's zombies are dead, to be sure, but the cause for their reanimation is more supernatural than biological. After a particle

ABOVE LEFT TO RIGHT:
Comedy-writer Max Brooks uses a fictional zombie war to showcase society's failings in this "oral history" inspired by Studs Terkel's *The Good War: An Oral History of World War II*. Coming soon to a theater near you.

Brian Keene's debut novel is often credited with sparking renewed interest in zombie literature post-2000.

The demon-zombies vs. humans war is in full swing in this sequel to *The Rising*, and the zombies are winning.

MONSTER ISLAND

DAVID WELLINGTON

'It's got all the stuff a zombie aficionado wants!' BoingBoing.net

MONSTER NATION

A ZOMBIE SEQUEL
DAVID WELLINGTON

"An instant horror classic." — BN.com

MONSTER PLANET

A ZOMBIE SEQUEL
DAVID WELLINGTON

LEFT TO RIGHT:
A prequel to *Monster Island*, *Monster Nation* explains the origins of Wellington's sentient zombies.

Twelve years after *Monster Island*, the dead have united and taken over, but the few remaining humans are still fighting.

accelerator experiment goes horribly wrong (as they do) and tears a hole in the fabric of the universe, demons from another dimension begin to possess the bodies of dead humans and animals. Because the cause of zombification is divorced from the dead body itself, these zombies possess all the intelligence and evilness of demons, as well as the memories of the host. Which, you may surmise, causes a few physical and emotional stresses for the intrepid survivors. This approach, which features a new breed of mindful dead, has become less unusual in the past decade; we've already seen a rise in zombies with consciousness in recent years in films such as *28 Weeks Later* (2007, although the "zombies" here were alive, albeit infected with a rage disease), *Colin* (2008), *Fido* (2006), and even in Romero's own *Land of the Dead* (2005). Keene followed this debut title with two more books in the series, *City of the Dead* (2005) and a collection of short stories set in *The Rising*'s universe called *The Rising: Selected Scenes from the End of the World* (2006).

David Wellington's popular zombie apocalypse trilogy—first published in serial form online,

beginning in 2004—takes a leaf from Keene's book. In *Monster Island*, the prequel *Monster Nation*, and the final chapter of *Monster Planet*, the zombies show a form of sentience despite being post-mortem in the more traditional sense. Wellington's imagining differs markedly from Brooks'; while *World War Z* presents a world overrun my zombies simply by virtue of their number and inability to be killed, *Monster Planet* gives us conscious zombies bent on world domination that mobilize as a group against the survivors. The effect is ultimately rather comedic, but it's a fun and entertaining story nonetheless.

Predictably, changes to pop-culture's definition of the zombie threat have kept pace with changes to society: the living dead have become everything from faster, smarter, and globally threatening to alive and, sometimes, technologically created— as in Stephen King's singular foray into zombie novels, *Cell* (2006). In King's zombie apocalypse, the undead are neither infected, irradiated, nor even truly dead; rather, a cell-phone-carried "pulse" turns all cell users into mindless killing machines. Or, at least, we're led to believe they're

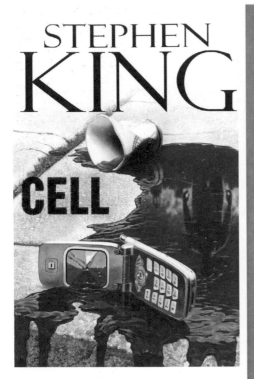

mindless, until they begin banding together into "flocks" and using their psychic powers on the unaffected survivors. King uses several indicators of the modern zombie incarnation—sentience, life, and speed—to characterize his zombies to bleak and moderately successful effect.

But zombies aren't all horrific downers in the twenty-first century. On the opposite end of the humor spectrum sits *The Stupidest Angel: A Heartwarming Tale of Christmas Terror* by adept satirical novelist Christopher Moore. The plot is fairly involved, but suffice it to say that when little Josh Barker sees Santa get murdered (actually his own father in a suit), he prays to God for a miracle to save Christmas. Enter idiotic Archangel Raziel, who grants Josh's wish and then some by reanimating the fake dead Santa as well as the rest of the deceased townspeople. Flesh-eating hilarity with a wry dose of Christmas cheer ensues.

Possibly the most influential zombie comedy written in the past several years is *Pride and*

Prejudice and Zombies, by Jane Austen and Seth Grahame-Smith. Essentially the original Austen novel with extra words about zombies inserted by Grahame-Smith, *Pride and Prejudice and Zombies* opened a whole new can of worms when in came repackaging, making scads of money off public domain classics. Although the book was published as recently as 2009, it has already inspired a graphic novel; a prequel *(Pride and Prejudice and Zombies: Dawn of the Dreadfuls,* 2010); and merchandise such as postcards, T-shirts, mugs, canvas art prints, and mousepads. A host of imitators followed, of course, bringing

ABOVE LEFT TO RIGHT:
Stephen King's only foray into zombie novels features cell-phone-induced rage and psychic powers. If he'd left it at rage this could have been considered nonfiction.

Christopher Moore often uses monsters to drive his satirical novels, but none of the others showcase a zombie Santa Claus.

PRIDE AND PREJUDICE AND ZOMBIES

BY JANE AUSTEN AND SETH GRAHAME-SMITH

THE *NEW YORK TIMES* BEST SELLER

The graphic novel based on the *New York Times* bestseller!

PRIDE AND PREJUDICE AND ZOMBIES

JANE AUSTEN AND SETH GRAHAME-SMITH

ADAPTED BY TONY LEE · ILLUSTRATED BY CLIFF RICHARDS

us *Sense and Sensibility and Sea Monsters* (2009), *Android Karenina* (2010), *Mansfield Park and Mummies* (2009), *Jane Slayre* (2010), and many, many more, either already published or currently planned, that are just too embarrassing to list. These mash-up novels are one-trick ponies at heart, and the fad will most likely soon fizzle out, but Grahame-Smith's original is an interesting exercise in updating classic literature to pander to modern tastes, and may even prompt more disaffected teenagers to find entertainment in the classics.

ABOVE LEFT TO RIGHT:
The only way to top a Jane Austen adaptation featuring a wet-shirted Colin Firth is to overrun Derbyshire with zombies.

The graphic novel version of Seth Grahame-Smith's mash-up novel, offering even more blood-stained Regency clothing for your viewing pleasure.

100 Zombie Fiction Titles

Since the publication of *Book of the Dead* in 1990, and more recently Max Brooks'
Zombie Survival Guide and Brian Keene's *The Rising*, the adult zombie fiction market has
exploded, with entire start-up publishers devoted to apocalyptic fiction featuring
the living dead. Here are just some of the titles available and upcoming, including
a few worthy young-adult efforts.

Autumn by David Moody (2010)

Autumn: The City by David Moody (2011)

Autumn: The Human Condition by David Moody (2005)

Autumn: The Purification by David Moody (2011)

Berserk by Tim Lebbon (2009)

Book of All Flesh by James Lowder, ed. (2001)

Book of the Dead by John Skipp and Craig Spector (1989)

Book of the Dead 2: Still Dead by John Skipp and Craig Spector (1992)

Book of Final Flesh by James Lowder, ed. (2003)

Book of More Flesh by James Lowder, ed. (2002)

Brains: A Zombie Memoir by Robin Becker (2010)

Breathers: A Zombie's Lament by S. G. Browne (2009)

The Breeze Horror by Candace Caponegro (1988)

Carrion by Gary Brandner (2001)

Cell: A Novel by Stephen King (2006)

City of the Dead by Brian Keene (2005)

Cluck: Murder Most Fowl by Eric D. Knapp (2001)

Coelbe by Eric S. Brown and Susan Brydenbaugh (2005)

Day by Day Armageddon by J. L. Bourne (2009)

Day by Day Armageddon 2: Beyond Exile by J. L. Bourne (2010)

The Dead by Mark E. Rogers (1989)

Deadfellas by David Whitman (2005)

The Deadlands by Scott A. Johnson (2005)

The Dead-Tossed Waves by Carrie Ryan (2010)

Dead America by Luke Kaloskie (2009)

Dead City by Joe McKinney (2006)

Dead Earth: The Green Dawn
      by Mark Justice and David Wilbanks (2010)

Dead Sea by Brian Keene (2007)

The Dead Shall Inherit the Earth by Vince Churchill (2001)

The Dead That Walk by Stephen Jones (2009)

Dead in the West by Joe R. Lansdale (1986)

Deathhunger by Bryan Smith (2009)

Death Walk by Matthew Sprange (2001)

The Devil's Plague by Mark Beynon (2010)

Dramatic of the Dead by Ian McKinnon (2009)

Down the Road: A Zombie Horror Story by Bowie Ibarra (2005)

Dying to Live: Life Sentence by Kim Paffenroth (2008)

Empire by David Dunwoody (2011)

Every Sigh, The End: A Novel About Zombies
      by Jason S. Hornsby (2007)

Ex-Heroes by Peter Clines (2010)

The Fog by James Herbert (2004)

The Forest of Hands and Teeth by Carrie Ryan (2009)

Generation Dead by Daniel Waters (2008)

Hater by David Moody (2009)

History Is Dead: A Zombie Anthology by Kim Paffenroth, ed. (2007)

I, Zombie by Curt Selby (1982)

Kiss of Life by Daniel Waters (2009)

The Living Dead: A Novel by George A. Romero (2010) (TBC)

Long Horn, Big Shaggy by Steve Vernon (2008)

The Mammoth Book of Zombies by Stephen Jones (1993)

Mondo Zombie by John Skipp, ed. (2006)

Monster Island by David Wellington (2006)

Monster Nation by David Wellington (2006)

Monster Planet by David Wellington (2007)

The New Dead: A Zombie Anthology by Christopher Golden, ed. (2010)

One Rainy Night by Richard Laymon (1991)

Patient Zero: A Joe Ledger Novel by Jonathan Maberry (2009)

Plague of the Dead by Z. A. Recht (2010)

Pride and Prejudice and Zombies by Seth Grahame-Smith (2009)

Pride and Prejudice and Zombies: Dawn of the Dreadfuls
      by Steve Hockensmith (2010)

The Queen by Eric S. Brown (2006)

Reign of the Dead by Len Barnhart (2005)

Reign of the Dead: Apocalypse End by Len Barnhart (2006)

Reign of the Dead: Outbreak by Len Barnhart (2005)

Resident Evil: Caliban Cove by S. D. Perry (1998)

Resident Evil: City of the Dead by S. D. Perry (1999)

Resident Evil: Code Veronica by S. D. Perry (2001)

Resident Evil: Nemesis by S. D. Perry (2000)

Resident Evil: The Umbrella Conspiracy by S. D. Perry (1998)

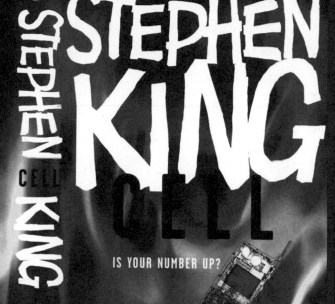

Resident Evil: Underworld by S. D. Perry (1999)
Resident Evil: Zero Hour by S. D. Perry (2004)
Resurrection Dreams by Richard Laymon (1988)
Risen by J. Knight (2002)
The Rising by Brian Keene (2004)
The Rising: Selected Scenes from the End of the World
    by Brian Keene (2009)
Rivers of Blood on Barbwire Vines by B.L. Snell (2008)
The Stephen Mr. Corpse by Jeff Strand (2004)
Stranger by Simon Clark (2002)
The Stupidest Angel: A Heartwarming Tale of Christmas Terror
    by Christopher Moore (2004)
Twilight of the Dead by Travis Adkins (2009)
The Undead zombie anthology
    by D.L. Snell and Eric S. Brown eds (2005)
The Undead: Vol 2. Skin and Bones
    by D.L. Snell and Travis Adkins (2006)
The Ultimate Zombie by Byron Preiss (ed.) (1993)
Valley of the Dead: The Truth Behind Dante's Inferno
    by Kim Paffenroth (2010)
The Zombie by Barclay Little (2008)
War Against the Zombies by Joseph Hirsch (2009)
War of the Worlds: The Blood, Guts and Zombies by Eric S. Brown (2009)

War Work by Philip Nutman (1991)
World War of the Dead: A Zombie Novel by Eric S. Brown (2009)
World War Z: An Oral History of the Zombie War by Max Brooks (2006)
Zombies by Walter Greatshell (2010)
Zombies: Apocalypse Rules by Walter Greatshell (2009)
Zombie Apocalypse! by Walter Greatshell (2010)
Zombies: Encounters with the Hungry Dead by John Skipp (ed.) (2009)
Zombies: A Record of the Year of Infection by Don Roff (2009)
Zombie Haiku: Good Poetry for Your... Brains by Ryan Mecum (2008)
Zombie Jam by David J. Schow (2003)
Zombie Love by Ray Garton (2010)
The Zombie Survival Guide: Complete Protection from the Living Dead
    by Max Brooks (2003)
Zombies vs. Unicorns by Holly Black and Justine Larbalestier
    (eds) (2010)

Interactive Evil:
Zombies in Video Games

Video games are a relatively new medium of entertainment, but zombies shambled their way onto the gaming scene from the outset, scarfing brains on eighties wunderkind home computer Commodore 64. An eponymous adaptation of Sam Raimi's hit flick *The Evil Dead* was released for the Commodore in 1984 (and later made its way onto the ZX Spectrum), wherein gamers played as an 8-bit version of Ash and battled the evil dead surrounded by the four walls of the film's infamous cabin. Also in 1984 came *Zombie Zombie*, from the maker of the innovative isometric 3D game *Ant Attack*, which featured a full-scale zombie apocalypse and a helicopter used to lure zombies to their deaths.

Already having a solid foothold in the gaming world, zombie games evolved along with available technology, and in 1994 the first-person shooter *Corpse Killer* was released for the Sega console, designed to be used with Sega's light gun (à la Nintendo's *Duck Hunt*). *Corpse Killer* features an unusual B-story in that the player's character has already been bitten and must delay his transformation with medicines while trying to stop the evil Dr. Hellman from releasing his zombie horde on the world. Unfortunately, the game's "interactive movie" construct—in which gameplay is meant to be as filmic as possible, with numerous live-action cutscenes and people in zombie costumes superimposed on live

FAR LEFT, BOTH IMAGES:
The adaptation of hit horror film *The Evil Dead* demonstrates the height of video game technology in 1984.

ABOVE: **From the creator of the highly regarded *Ant Attack* came cutting-edge isometric-projection zombies designed for the earliest personal computers, in *Zombie Zombie*.**

ABOVE: **LucasArts can do no wrong, and its beloved, trans-generational *Monkey Island* series fanned its own flames by making LeChuck the Pirate a zombie in the series' second installment.**

RIGHT: **Interactive movie-style game *Corpse Killer* featured a jungle zombie infestation. Sadly, it was an innovative idea hobbled by subpar execution.**

backgrounds—was already waning in popularity. *Corpse Killer*'s unintentionally humorous zombies and limited gameplay only garnered it mixed reviews at best.

The early nineties saw several zombie-themed first-person shooters hit the market, including LucasArts' brilliant B-movie homage *Zombies Ate My Neighbors* (1993) and its lesser-known sequel, *Ghoul Patrol*, released the following year. (*Monkey Island 2* also featured an undead antagonist in the form of LeChuck the Pirate.) But it wasn't until the first installment of Capcom's new zombie series *Resident Evil* hit shelves in 1996 that the walking dead shuffled into gamers' hearts and became a permanent fixture in fifth-generation consoles, as well as their successors.

Developed for the Sony Playstation, *Resident Evil* took the standard plotless shoot-'em-up zombie game to new heights. Set in the fictional town of Raccoon City, reports of strange murders and cannibalistic behavior prompt the local police department to deploy the Special Tactics and Rescue Service. The Bravo team disappears in the field without a trace, so Alpha team is flown in to investigate. After finding Bravo team's deserted landing site and helicopter, Alpha team are set upon by vicious dogs and are abandoned by their own helicopter pilot. The remaining members of the team take refuge in a nearby mansion, which they assume is disused, but instead they find it populated by murderous,

mutated humans, plants, and animals, which have all been infected by the zombie-making T-virus. In order to survive, the team must solve the mystery of the house without being eaten during the process.

Often dubbed the first "survival horror" game, *Resident Evil* combined exciting third-person shooter gameplay with adventure-style puzzles and innovative strategy demands. Of course, in 1996, *any* demands for strategy by a zombie-themed game were unusual, innovative or otherwise. This game predated the advent of voiceovers by proper actors, so, predictably, much of the voice acting is pretty dismal. But the beautifully rendered settings and creatures, the spot-on horrific atmosphere, and the mysterious storyline that gives out as much as the player puts in, more than make up for its few failings, which are mainly due to conventions of its time anyway. More to the point, *Resident Evil* was the first zombie game that came across as genuinely scary. From that first in-play cutscene where our intrepid player-character comes face-to-protruding eyeball with an undead scientist, gasping gamers realized they were onto something special. And clearly so did Capcom, as the franchise continues to this day.

Resident Evil 2 and *3* were released in quick succession before the millennial turnover, and took the characters out of the mansion and into Raccoon City, exploring the wider consequences of the T-virus' dissemination. *Resident Evil Code:*

ABOVE LEFT TO RIGHT:
From the game just that won't die, Capcom remakes its seminal *Resident Evil*, widely considered the progenitor of the "survival horror" genre, for a new generation of fans.

***Resident Evil: Code Veronica* attempts to make the flattop cool again . . . and fails.**

***Resident Evil Zero* allows players to "partner zap" between these fine young characters, each with their own gameplay advantages.**

This sequel opened up the gameplay to include crowds and open spaces, in contrast to the earlier, more contained *Resident Evil* settings.

OPPOSITE TOP TO BOTTOM:
In *Resident Evil 5*, when the zombies start picking up chainsaws, it's time to forsake your military overlords.

***Resident Evil 5*: too late!**

Veronica (2000), while considered part of the main series, is both the first game to move the setting outside of Raccoon City (to an Umbrella Corporation facility in Paris) and to use true 3D background graphics. Gameplay remained largely the same as the first three in the series, however, and didn't change much for *Resident Evil Zero*, a prequel brought out in 2002, either. It wasn't until *Resident Evil 4* (2005) that the Capcom wizards changed the entire system of gameplay and hired trained actors to provide the voiceovers. Instead of focusing on the mad biological exploits of the Umbrella Corporation, the player-character Leon S. Kennedy from *Resident Evil 2* is sent on a mission to rescue the President of the United States' daughter. The enemy is a more evolved sort of zombie, comprising infected humans with quick reflexes and the ability to organize and communicate (bringing the video game conception of the zombie more in line with the trends already seen in movies and literature). *Resident Evil 4* attracted widespread critical acclaim and is now one of the top-rated zombie games of all time. As such, Capcom show no signs of abandoning *Resident Evil* any time soon; the seventh installment, *Resident Evil 5*, was released in 2009, becoming the series' bestselling title, and rumors are circulating that the planned *Resident Evil 6* will be a full reboot of the franchise.

At the same time *Resident Evil* was staging its gaming revolution, Sega fell back on the tried-and-true, rail-shooter format for its own zombie franchise, *House of the Dead*. First released in 1996 as an arcade game, *House*'s storylines are simple (and largely irrelevant), since the gameplay relies solely on gallery-style shooting along a predetermined linear path. Which isn't to say it's not worth a play, since mindless gun violence is

CLOCKWISE FROM BOTTOM LEFT:
The second sequel in this popular first-person-shooter franchise measures how fast players kill zombies, as well as how accurate they are, adding a new dimension to gameplay.

House of the Dead: Overkill **is a prequel to the original game but is also the most graphically violent out of all the games.**

In the alternate-reality, *Evil Dead* **"sequel"** *Regeneration*, **Ash fights zombies in an asylum for the criminally insane. Enough said.**

one of the cornerstones of arcade games, and the bosses are as original and challenging as they can be within the format. The first *House of the Dead* was popular enough to spawn three sequels and four spin-off game titles, including the Louisiana-based prequel *House of the Dead: Overkill* released in 2009, as well as two excremental film adaptations. The first film, *House of the Dead* (2003), directed by everyone's favorite horror underdog Uwe Boll, is currently considered one of the worst films of all time. Give the movies a wide berth, and spend a few unproductive hours playing the games instead.

Resident Evil may be acknowledged as one of the most important games ever made for its invention of the "survival horror" genre, but it also inspired a number of zombified imitators. More *Evil Dead* games were generated for the sixth-generation consoles between 2000 and 2005, but one of the real stand-out games, *Dead Rising* (also by zombie aficionados Capcom), was developed for the seventh-generation Xbox 360 in 2006. Based very heavily on the zombie films of George A. Romero—particularly *Dawn of the Dead*—*Dead Rising* follows player-character Frank West, a photojournalist, who finds himself trapped in a mall in the zombie-infested town of Willamette, Colorado. Frank must of course fight his way through the zombie horde while trying to discover the cause of the outbreak. Designed as a "sandbox" game, *Dead Rising*

allows for enormous flexibility in gameplay, with multiple endings depending on players' actions (or inactions) during the game. One of its most interesting aspects involves the vast number of weapons available for use within the mall—it's not unusual to beat a zombie to death with a cash register, blind it with a traffic cone, or stab it with a tricked-out toy lightsaber. *Dead Rising*'s flexibility and humorous side notes have made it a hit with zombie gamers, leading it to be ported to the Nintendo Wii (*Dead Rising: Chop Till You Drop*, 2009), and a sequel is currently in development.

Survival horror is considered more forward-thinking of the games featuring the undead out there, but once the first-person-shooter zombie game went cooperative, as it has in Valve's *Left 4 Dead* series, things got a lot more interesting. Set in a post-apocalyptic America, *Left 4 Dead* features four immune survivors who are forced to make their way through hordes of infected to reach safety. The gameplay is set up in short, geographic goal-oriented campaigns, prompting players to fight though several landscapes, from urban to country, as they progress through the game.

Left 4 Dead's zombies are far more *28 Days Later* in origin than *Night of the Living Dead*, as the creatures are infected with a rabies-like virus and are very much alive. The most common zombie in the game is quick on its feet and sometimes travels in packs, which isn't anything

ABOVE LEFT: **As photojournalist Frank, *Dead Rising* players fight the hordes on their way to the Orange Julius stand.**

ABOVE: **Based loosely on Romero's *Dawn of the Dead*, *Dead Rising* allows players to smash up zombies with common household appliances.**

ABOVE: **Concept art for Left 4 Dead 2: the morning commute is going to be a real bitch.**

FAR LEFT: **Left 4 Dead combined the first-person shooter with cooperative multiplayer gameplay to great effect, proving that the most deadly in-game foe of them all is the player's own friends.**

LEFT: **Left 4 Dead 2: they just want to be loved.**

we haven't seen before. However, Valve took their modern zombie concept one step further by including "special" infected, such as the Boomer that spits blinding bile and the crying, berserker Witch. In addition, though the gameplay is fairly linear, the game's A.I. system is flexible enough to modify attack points and item pickups based on players' achievements, so that each campaign can be played several times to different effect.

These extra touches added a new dimension to zombie play, and this, combined with fully realized settings, atmospheric music, filmic constructs, and the ability to campaign against friends as zombie attackers has garnered Left 4 Dead accolades from players and critics alike.

Of course, such success can only spell "sequel," and Left 4 Dead 2 was released in late 2009

and features four new survivors traveling from Savannah, Georgia, to New Orleans, Louisiana, in an attempt to find rescue. Gameplay is similar to the first game (and is constructed on the same engine), but Valve have added melee weapons, in addition to the time-honored firearms, as well as several new special infected. The narrative is smoother and more connected between campaigns, and there's a wider variety of settings, like the genuinely creepy abandoned amusement park and a depressingly overrun survivors' shanty town in the bayou. Valve also managed to up the gore and violence quotient, resulting in bans in Germany and Australia. Despite (or more likely because of) this, *Left 4 Dead 2* has become another hit with zombie fans, and for good reason.

Since the mid-nineties, zombie-themed video games have been steadily increasing in popularity and quality, and they show no sign of disappearing into the ether anytime soon. In 2009 alone the gaming gods gifted us with *Alive 4-Ever*; *Burn, Zombie Burn!*; *Call of Duty: World at War: Zombies*; *Fort Zombie*; *I Made a Game with Zombies in It!*; *Plants vs. Zombies*; *Shellshock 2: Blood Trails*; *Zombie Apocalypse*; and *Zombie Driver*, to name but a few. From the simplest cell-phone application to A.I.-enhanced console games, zombies have infected the brains of gaming culture and left us with this scintillating conclusion: "Itchy. Tasty."

The Zombie Invasion: Music of the Dead

With the birth of punk rock in the mid-seventies, followed closely by its flamboyant little sister goth, it's hardly surprising that fringe musicians early on would mine equally anti-establishment horror films to further their anarchic imagery. It began as early as 1977, in fact.

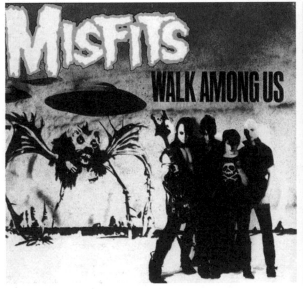
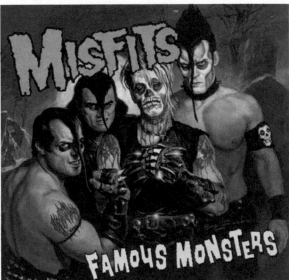

Glenn Danzig's punk band The Misfits is often credited with creating the "horror punk" musical subgenre, as their music is riddled with sci-fi and horror B-movie references. Even their label Plan 9 Records, created after they were unable to find one interested enough to release their albums, pays homage to Ed Wood's classic cult sci-fi film *Plan 9 from Outer Space*. The Misfits' style was an intimidating mix of punk, goth, and rockabilly; bassist Jerry Only is credited with inventing his own horror-punk hairstyle, the appropriately named "devilock." As the group drew heavily on influences from kitsch horror films of the fifties, sixties, and seventies, zombies inevitably crop up in their songs. Their second album *Walk Among Us* (released in 1982 after their first, *Static Age*,

was shelved), features such tracks as "Night of the Living Dead" (inspired by Romero's film of the same name), "Astro Zombies," and "Braineaters." *Earth A.D.*, their third and last album with Danzig before he defected to find heavy metal stardom, continues the horror imagery and lyrics, with even darker undertones, faster riffs, and demonic-leaning lyrics. The Misfits continue to this day without Danzig; notably, "Scream!," a song from their 1999 album *Famous Monsters*, has an accompanying video directed by Romero, which showcases the band members dressed as zombies and attacking a hospital.

45 Grave, formed in 1979, also stands out as one of the early progenitors of horror punk and had

ABOVE LEFT TO RIGHT:
The Misfits' first full-length album release, after they'd moved squarely into the horror-punk camp.

Released almost twenty years after *Walk Among Us*—well after Glenn Danzig had left the band—the Misfits keep horror punk alive. One track was turned into a music video by George Romero.

BELOW: **Michael Jackson and his date (Ola Ray) come under attack from a group of zombies in "Thriller."**

BOTTOM: **The now iconic choreography in "Thriller" has been mimicked on dance floors worldwide, including the unlikely stage of a Philippines prison yard.**

their 1983 song "Partytime" included on the soundtrack for *Return of the Living Dead*. These two bands in particular have influenced myriad horror-inspired bands, including the Serpenteens, Rosemary's Babies, American Werewolves, Balzac, and The Independents. But, possibly more importantly, it was the groundbreaking horror-punk bands like The Misfits and 45 Grave that set a precedent by bridging the gap between popular music and horror films, setting the stage for future collaborations, the most successful of which is the 1983 music video for Michael Jackson's hit single, "Thriller" (see also p. 90).

Horror punk has always been an underground movement, but zombies in music truly hit the mainstream in the "Thriller" video. Directed by John Landis—of *An American Werewolf in London* and *Twilight Zone: The Movie* fame—"Thriller" is a fourteen-minute short horror masterpiece, featuring voiceover narration by the legend that is Vincent Price, as well as special make-up effects by the equally legendary Rick Baker. If you're reading this book there's no doubt you're aware of the video's content already, so suffice it to say that in 2009 "Thriller" became the first music video to be selected for the Library of Congress' National Film Registry, which chooses films that are "'culturally, historically, or aesthetically' significant to be preserved for all time." Of "Thriller," the Registry noted, "The most famous music video of all time . . . Michael Jackson revolutionized the music industry with this lavish and expensive production." And, don't forget, he did it with *zombies*. It's doubtful the video would have made such waves if it didn't feature the dancing undead—zombies (and often horror in general) may be considered lowbrow by the unenlightened, but they're nothing if not popular.

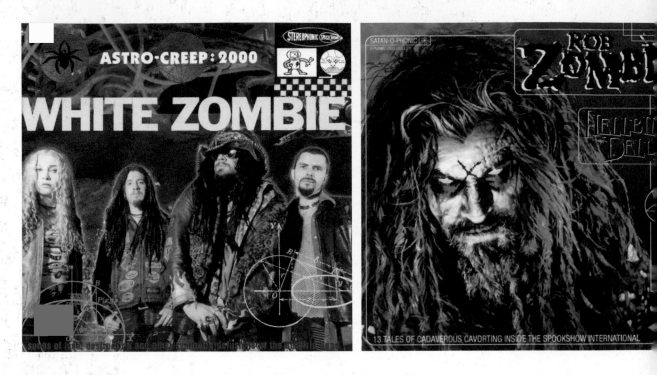

Of course, it would be remiss if we didn't mention Rob Cummings, better known to the music world as Rob Zombie. Zombie founded the band White Zombie in 1985, which became popular for its heavy metal guitar riffs overlaid with horror-inspired lyrics and imagery. Though their music was rife with zombie references, White Zombie's most popular song proved to be "More Human than Human" from their 1995 album *Astro-Creep: 2000*. Inspired by classic cult film *Blade Runner*, the song spawned a music video that is intercut with images of graveyards, clowns, and other spooky iconography. It would be the first directorial effort from Rob Zombie. After White Zombie disbanded, Rob Zombie embarked on a solo career continuing White Zombie's tradition of horror-inspired metal, but he also found time to set himself up as a horror film director. Though he has yet to make a zombie film proper, his debut *House of 100 Corpses* features a few lively cadavers in the subterranean caverns of the monstrous Firefly family homestead.

One of the funniest and most zombified bands of recent years has got to be The Zombeatles,

a parody of The Beatles … but dressed as zombies. Talk about high concept. Formed in 2004 by a few members of Madison-based band The Gomers, The Zombeatles were never meant to be perennially popular; they intended to appear at Halloween time for a few theme shows only, and then hibernate for the rest of the year until resurrected again for seasonal laughs. But in 2006 they made a music video for their spoof song "A Hard Day's Night of the Living Dead," which was soon noticed and disseminated by none other than horror aficionado Rob Zombie himself, resulting in widespread fame and demand for the Fab Gore. The band followed up their hit video with a short film titled, *The Zombeatles: All You Need Is Brains*, and they now tour all year as their rotting alter egos.

Even in music zombies provide an almost unprecedented flexibility for horror fans—they can be anything from harsh, anti-establishment social commentary to mainstream entertainment to a novelty joke.

ABOVE LEFT: **White Zombie's final album release, featuring the extraordinarily popular track "More Human than Human." Also included is the undead-themed track, "I, Zombie."**

ABOVE: **After Rob Zombie disbanded White Zombie, he continued the tradition he started with this theatrical horror-themed release.**

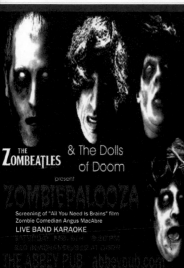

THE ZOMBEATLES & The Dolls of Doom

present

ZOMBIEPALOOZA

Screening of "All You Need Is Brains" film
Zombie Comedian Angus MacAbre
LIVE BAND KARAOKE

THE ABBEY PUB abbeypub.com

THE ZOMBEATLES EAT ALL THE BRATS

TOP: A part of the Zombeatles' vast (and mostly fictional) discography.

MIDDLE LEFT: Once intended to be a Halloween-only act, The Zombeatles now play live year round.

ABOVE: The Zombeatles play their greatest hits on stage in zombie make-up and the requisite Beatles wigs.

LEFT: The Zombeatles' first—and so far only—album includes Beatles- parody tracks such as "I Wanna Eat Your Hand" and "Hey Food."

153

Zombie Walks: A Growing Epidemic

In the early 2000s, a new menace took to the streets to harrass humanity, joining leaflet hawkers and tourists who stop suddenly in the middle of rush-hour pedestrian traffic. But these interlopers are of a different breed—they shuffle slowly along the sidewalks, moaning for brains and clawing at any living flesh that passes them by. Well, maybe they aren't so different from the average commuter after all.

It all began with horror fans organizing to promote events or their interest in the undead. One of the first zombie walks aimed to promote a film festival in Sacramento, California, while a very small gathering in Toronto in 2003 was staged purely to celebrate the participants' love of the living dead phenomemon. But as films, games, and books featuring zombies increased in popularity, so has the incidence and number of people dressing like ghouls for business and pleasure.

All of the walks feature a group of men, women, and sometimes children in zombie make-up and ragged clothing who unleash themselves on a public place, with some kind of structure to their group, to spread the joy of shambling about in a crowd. However, some walk organizers push the creativity boundaries a little more, just to keep passersby on their toes, in turn elevating the zombie walk close to the level of performance art. As such, the walks are now apt to feature members dressed as soldiers or riot police, called in to contain the outbreak, and—in an interactive theater twist—some walks plant onlookers in the gathering civilian crowds, who are then attacked and turned into zombies by the walkers. By breaking the fourth wall in such a manner, the walks become both more fun and seemingly more dangerous for hapless bystanders. Also, in moving steadily more toward a performance art model, many walks are staged as spoof political rallies, demanding zombie rights among other things. Of course, the ubiquitous "zombie pub crawl" model is also very popular, if less socially aware.

ABOVE: **A Zombie Nazi mingles with the participants of the 2009 Toronto Zombie Walk. Photo by Dash Revery.**

Though the simple love of horror and the undead is a driving factor in staging zombie walks, never let it be said that horror fans don't have social consciences; many walks have been organized to benefit charities, incorporating such socially advantageous aspects as food drives (get it?!), fundraising for cancer and other medical research, and support for troops.

Zombie walks appear to have started in North America, but they have begun to grow into a truly global phenomenon in the past decade. Walks have been successfully staged in Australia and all over the UK, with thousands of people turning up for the events. The Big Chill Festival in the UK currently holds the Guiness World Record for largest zombie gathering on official record, attracting more than four thousand zombies to the August 2009 festival (though a later,

unverified gathering in Michigan in 2009 claims eight thousand participants).

Zombie walks are getting larger and more frequent as more people discover the joy of zomming up and helping out. Several websites are now dedicated to bringing zombie walk enthusiasts together, so do a little research and then suit up and stumble out to show undead solidarity on the streets of your hometown.

Locate a zombie walk near you:
www.zombiewalk.com
www.crawlofthedead.com
www.terror4fun.co.uk
www.torontozombiewalk.ca

CLOCKWISE FROM ABOVE: **No laughing matter: the 2009 Toronto Zombie Walk sends in the clown. Photo by Dash Revery.**

This prom king has seen better days. Photo by Dash Revery.

Hordes of ravenous zombies mass at the 7th Annual Zombie Walk in Toronto, 2009. Photo by Lara Willis.

Zombies on the Small Screen

Just like in film, zombies have been popping up in television for decades. Only a year after Romero's *Night of the Living Dead* invaded movie theaters, everyone's favorite gothic soap opera, *Dark Shadows* (1966–71), featured a B-storyline in which one of the main characters, Quentin Collins, is turned into a shambling, moaning, undead wreck. However, the *Dark Shadows* version of a zombie differs somewhat from Romero's; while Quentin is killed and brought back to life, he is also able to be cured of his magical zombie curse and is restored to full humanity, harkening back to the voodoo-based origins popular in earlier films such as Victor Halperin's *White Zombie* (1932) and Jacques Tourneur's *I Walked with a Zombie* (1943).

Similar to *Dark Shadows*, television shows with a supernatural bent have tended to feature zombies in some episodes, while not making them a fixture of the overall narrative. Both *Buffy the Vampire Slayer* and its spin-off series *Angel* had episodes that focused on the living dead in the late 1990s and early 2000s, but within their fictional universe zombies were clearly defined as the deceased reanimated by magic; Frankenstein's monster-types, brought back to life by scientific means, were not considered true zombies. Often the zombies in *Buffy* and *Angel* were indistinguishable from their living selves—apart from the smell—but the mindless, murderous Romero template appeared as well.

In 2005, *Doctor Who* presented an interesting twist on the zombie with its Hugo Award–winning two-episode story arc "The Empty Child" and "The Doctor Dances." Due to a sort of "alien infection"—or nanogenes recreating humans based on a single prototype—men, women, and children are transformed into gas-mask-wearing zombies with the single purpose of finding the prototype's lost mother. Though not your typical zombies, the recreated humans in these episodes have much in common with the Romero version: they're dead (since the prototype was a corpse), they can "infect" humans through physical contact, they have strength and abilities beyond that of normal

ABOVE LEFT TO RIGHT:
In the *Masters of Horror* episode "Dance of the Dead," cattle prods are used to reanimate zombies for business and pleasure.

A bouncer neither condones nor condemns zombie theft in "Dance of the Dead."

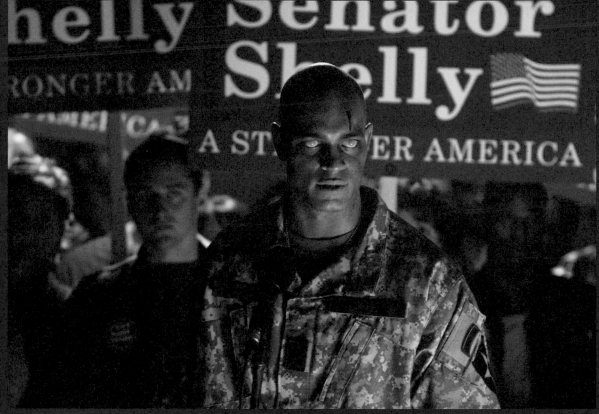

protagonists). The third episode, "Dance of the Dead," was directed by Tobe Hooper—based on a short story by Richard Matheson—and it takes place in a post-apocalyptic America where victims of biological warfare animate in a sort of dance post-mortem with the help of an electrical current. These zombies don't eat human flesh and aren't particularly violent, but they are used for rather grim entertainment by depraved survivors. As such, Hooper employs them more as a means of social commentary than horror foes, which nicely complements Joe Dante's sixth episode of the series, "Homecoming."

humans, and they are monomaniacal in their need and search for a specific thing (in this case, it's some mysterious mother figure as opposed to the usual brains or human flesh).

On the other hand, *Masters of Horror*, which ran for two seasons from 2005–2007 on Showtime, was set up to be more a series of stand-alone, one-hour movies than an episodic television show, and several of its installments used zombies as the prime antagonists (and often

"Homecoming" aired during George W. Bush's second term in office, and the episode is rife with commentary. Set in the U.S. during a difficult foreign war—and only one month before a presidential election—the incumbent president's head speechwriter wishes on live television that the men killed in the current

ABOVE: **In the *Masters of Horror* story "Homecoming," if you hate zombies, you hate America.**

LEFT: **Master of Horror Joe Dante imparts directorial wisdom on the set of "Homecoming."**

157

ABOVE: **Zombies are rounded up and placed in military camps in the *Masters of Horror* segment "Homecoming."**

conflict could come back to life and tell the people what they think of the war. And taking a leaf out of W.W. Jacobs' classic ghost story "The Monkey's Paw," that's exactly what they do. Only the dead soldiers from the current war arise, and like "Dance of the Dead," they are non-violent, but unlike that episode, they retain all their memories and their personalities from when they were alive. Moreover, in another departure from the Romero archetype, they feel pain, and they can't be killed by any means, including a shot to the head. The American public soon discovers that the only way to rid themselves of these zombie soldiers is to let them vote, after which they simply fall dead (seriously) to the ground. Unfortunately for America, the Republicans in the story are reprehensible enough to screw even undead servicemen, which then triggers a full-scale zombie takeover of Capitol Hill.

"Haeckel's Tale," based on a Clive Barker short story and directed by John McNaughton (of

Henry: Portrait of a Serial Killer fame), walks a similar path to the above in that zombies are mostly utilized to show how much more horrible the living can be. In true Clive Barker fashion, sex and death are intertwined when elderly Wolfram, who is physically incapable of satisfying his wife Elise's carnal urges, pays a necromancer to raise the dead—including her former husband—in a nearby cemetery to have sex with Elise. Soon Elise develops a taste for the undead, going so far as to bear and rear a zombie baby and sit idly by as her current husband and would-be (living) lover are killed. McNaughton's zombies have many traditional characteristics—they're dead, rotting, slow, and mostly mindless—although they retain some aspects of their former selves (namely devotion to Elise). In a complete reversal, the seventh episode of the second season, "The Screwfly Solution," nods more to the infected raging zombies seen in *28 Days Later* (2002) than the Romero archetype. Adapted from a story by science-fiction author Alice Sheldon (aka James

Tiptree Jr.) and directed by Joe Dante, "The Screwfly Solution" doesn't feature any of Dante's typical comedy elements (as in, for example, the "Homecoming" episode). Instead, we have a global infection that only affects men, driving them to kill when sexually aroused. Of course, this means that most of their victims are women, and "Screwfly" focuses on the effect of this femicide. The infected men are still alive but incapable of controlling their irrational, homicidal urges, and they eventually wipe out the Earth's entire female population. Despite being terribly dark and depressing, Dante has given us yet another conception of the modern zombie: infected and raging, yes, but neither dead nor mindless, as the men retain their former personalities except when in the throes of sexual excitement.

After *30 Days of Night* writer Steve Niles helped reinvigorate the vampire craze, he turned his hand to zombies with an episode for NBC's television horror anthology *Fear Itself*. Being a watered-down broadcast version of *Masters of Horror*, *Fear Itself* only lasted eight episodes (five more were produced that never aired), but it was long enough to broadcast the zombie-themed "New Year's Day," directed by Darren Lynn Bousman (of the *Saw* film franchise), based on a short story by Paul Kane, and adapted for the screen by Steve Niles and Ben Sokolowski. "New Year's Day" is notable for its perspective more than its quality, in that the entire episode is actually shot from the zombies' point of view, postulating that—despite being undead, groaning, and

murderous—zombies still think they're human and just want to find love like the rest of us. It's a real tearjerker.

While most zombie TV has been limited to supernatural shows with periodic appearances, or horror series with single zombie-themed episodes, Charlie Brooker's *Dead Set* (2008) comprised an entire five-episode series about a zombie apocalypse. Set in a *Big Brother*–style reality show compound, the contestants are oblivious while a zombie outbreak outside the house wipes out most of the population of Britain. *Dead Set*'s zombies are a combination of the Romero archetype and the new *28-Days-Later*-type: while they are definitely dead and mindless, they are also agile and capable of running. It's only a matter of time before the infection invades the house, but the real terror here is that we're left wondering whether the Earth is going to have to be repopulated by the offspring of reality-show contestants.

And television isn't nearly done with zombies yet. In late 2010, AMC aired an episodic adaptation of Robert Kirkman's smash-hit comic series *The Walking Dead*, created by Frank Darabont (*The Shawshank Redemption, The Mist)*, who wrote and directed the pilot. Hopes for this were high among horror and comics fans alike, who reasoned that if it did well, it might provide the catalyst needed to spark an undead revolution on television, similar to what we've seen in film during the first decade of the new millennium.

Rotten Between the Panels: EC and the Golden Age of Horror Comics

William Gaines has a lot to answer for. After he took over his father's company, Educational Comics, in 1947, Gaines attempted to continue the publisher's legacy of innocuous American history and Bible stories, but before the decade was out he began publishing fiction stories in the romance, crime, and western genres among others. It wasn't until 1950, however, that Gaines began publishing the stories that would bring him the most notoriety and help cause a moral implosion in the comics industry; those titles were, of course, in the horror genre.

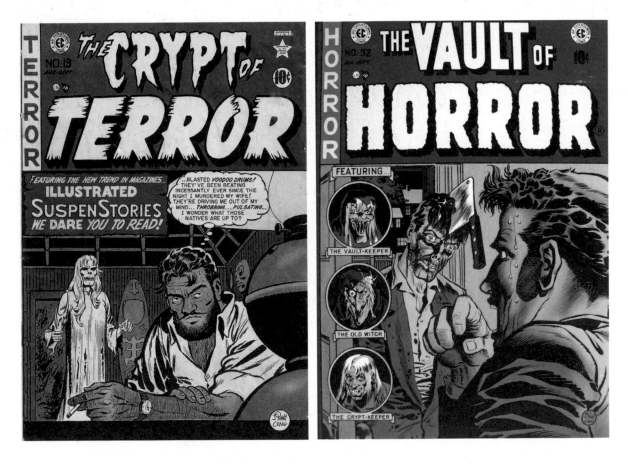

ABOVE: **This 1950 issue of** *The Crypt of Terror* **boasts a Johnny Craig cover featuring two vital elements in any zombie story: a walking corpse, and a hefty dose of voodoo.**

ABOVE RIGHT: **Johnny Craig's cover for the August/September 1953 issue of** *The Vault of Horror* **proved a little too gory even by EC's standards, and was censored at the time. Shown here is the restored, reprinted version.**

FEATURING...

THE CRYPT-KEEPER

THE OLD WITCH

THE VAULT-KEEPER

In 1950 two previously crime-centered titles, *Crime Patrol* and *War against Crime*, were repackaged and relaunched as *Crypt of Terror* and *Vault of Horror*, respectively. After just three issues, *Crypt of Terror* was again renamed *Tales from the Crypt*, probably the most famous and enduring horror comic of all time, thanks in no small part to the HBO television show of the same name (1989–96), which featured modernized adaptations of original EC material from the fifties. Horror proved hugely popular with the comics-buying public, and more titles followed hot on the heels of *Vault* and *Crypt*, including

The Haunt of Fear (previously *Gunfighter*, a western) and *Shock SuspenStories*. Gaines and his right-hand editor Al Feldstein demonstrated their business and creative savvy by hiring extraordinarily talented artists of the day, such as Johnny Craig, Frank Franzetta, Basil Wolverton, Reed Crandall, and Jack Davis, and giving them an almost unprecedented amount of creative freedom. As a result, EC Comics' horror lines produced frightening stories that were well told and beautifully illustrated; they were also, lest we forget, gruesome and nasty as hell.

ABOVE: **A corpse digs himself out of his own grave in this Jack Davis cover art for EC's *Tales from the Crypt* #37 (1953).**

STORY BY ARTHUR PORGES   ART BY JOE ORLANDO

The supernatural figured heavily in all of EC's horror lines, often as a catalyst or punishment for the evil that men do, and zombies were no exception. Often acting as instruments of revenge or protection, EC Comics' zombies were generally magical in origin and—as one would expect from a comic that prided itself on graphic depictions of gore and violence—displayed their rotting flesh to the best advantage. Although these magical origins were often the result of unspecified curses, voodoo did make several appearances right from the inception of the comics, including "Zombie!" (*Tales from the Crypt* 19, 1950), "A Fatal Caper!" (*Tales from the Crypt* 20, 1950), "Busted Marriage!" (*Tales from the Crypt* 35, 1953), "Half-Way Horrible!" (*Vault of Horror* 26, 1952), and "'Til Death" (*Vault of Horror* 28, 1953—demonstrating rare exclamation point restraint) to name just a few.

In fact, zombies were so popular in EC Comics' horror lines (as well as those of EC's imitators), that when the Comics Code Authority instated its genre-comic–killing "Comics Code" in 1954,

LEFT TOP: **The 1964 debut issue of Warren Publishing's successor title to the EC horror comics, *Creepy*, featured a zombie tale, "Voodoo," as its very first story, as related by writers Russ Jones and Bill Pearson and artist Joe Orlando.**

LEFT BOTTOM: **The first issue of *Creepy* boasted a second zombie story, as murdered comic strip artists return from the dead in the "The Success Story."**

Images © 2010 New Comic Company

zombies were specifically mentioned as a forbidden subject, along with other popular horror archetypes: "Scenes dealing with, or instruments associated with walking dead, torture, vampires and vampirism, ghouls, cannibalism, and werewolfism are prohibited" (General Standards Part B, Section 5). That, along with banning the use of the terms "horror" and "terror" in comic book titles and prohibiting "all scenes of horror" and "lurid, unsavory, gruesome illustrations," pretty much ended the heyday of horror comics in the 1950s, but it wouldn't be too long before EC's legacy rose from the dead to walk again, as it were.

Meanwhile, Warren Publishing found a way to circumvent the Comics Code in the 1960s by releasing its horror comics in black-and-white magazine format. *Creepy* launched in 1964, followed by *Eerie* two years later and *Vampirella*

in 1969 (though in 1970 Vampirella herself transformed from a simple horror host to a character in her own right, abandoning the horror anthology format). Using many of the visionary artists from the EC stable—Franzetta, Craig, and Crandall—plus a host of new (or new to horror, or just new to *Creepy*) talent including Neal Adams, Steve Ditko, and Bernie Wrightson, *Creepy* and its offspring followed the winning EC formula of well-illustrated ghoulish stories, mining the depths of horror monsters—including zombies on a fairly frequent basis. But both *Creepy* and *Eerie* folded in 1983 after Warren went bankrupt.

EC Comics' Film Revival

Less than twenty years after William Gaines ceased publication on all EC Comics' genre titles, apart from Code-proof *Mad* magazine, British horror film production company Amicus released *Tales from the Crypt* (1972), a portmanteau of five linked stories based on original EC Comics' plots. The film features a subdued (read: less punning) version of EC's iconic "GhouLunatic" the Crypt Keeper, and three of the five tales showcase the dead coming back to life. In "Reflection of Death" (*Tales from the Crypt* 23, 1951), a man wakes up after a car accident thinking he's alive, but learns differently when people run screaming from him; "Poetic Justice" (*The Haunt of Fear* 12, 1952) tells the story of an old man who, after being driven to suicide by cruel neighbors, returns from the dead a year later to exact his revenge; and "Wish You Were Here" (*The Haunt of Fear* 22, 1953) is yet another zombified retelling of W.W. Jacobs' classic story "The Monkey's Paw," just going to show that wishing the dead back to life never, ever ends well, but we're sure glad people keep doing it.

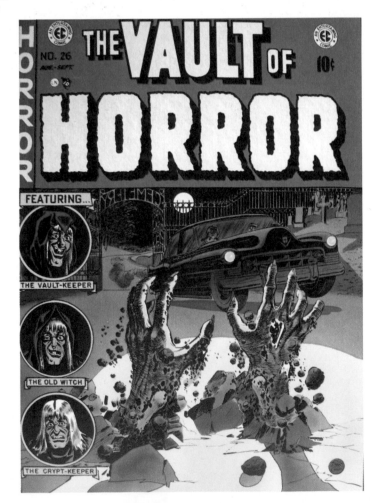

A year after *Tales from the Crypt*, Amicus brought out another horror anthology film based on EC horror lines, this time named after a different but equally famous title, *The Vault of Horror* (1973). *Vault* featured a wider variety of stories but no zombies per se—audiences would have to wait until 1982's *Creepshow*, a horror/comedy anthology directed by zombie aficionado George Romero and written by master of the horror novel Stephen King.

Creepshow's tales are not directly based on EC Comics' plots but are rather original and adapted King stories written as homages to EC's enduring brand of outré horror. As such, poetic (in)justice features heavily as a theme, and often the

wronged party returns from the grave to exact revenge. In "Father's Day," a murdered patriarch comes back from the dead to murder his money-grubbing relatives and, more importantly, to get a piece of the Father's Day cake he was denied on the night of his death seven years before (although he did kind of deserve to die, seeing as he had his own son-in-law assassinated); two lovers return from a watery grave to avenge their deaths at the hand of the woman's cuckolded husband in "Something to Tide You Over"; and the epilogue to the wraparound story, while not expressly featuring zombies, does play with the trappings of voodoo. The stories in *Creepshow* are suitably over-the-top in classic EC style—often verging on the absurd—but the sequel, *Creepshow 2* (1987), another portmanteau based on stories by King and adapted for the screen by Romero, has one of the most hilarious and cringe-worthy representations of the revenge zombie ever to hit celluloid. In "The Hitchhiker," wealthy, self-involved Annie oversleeps in her

gigolo's bed, and realizes she'll have to get home in a hurry to greet her husband and avoid suspicion. She speeds along the dark roads and accidently hits and kills a hitchhiker. Not wanting her extramarital affair exposed, Annie simply takes off, since there were no witnesses, A short time later she briefly pulls over to the side of the road to wrestle with her defective conscience, giving the now-undead hitchhiker an opportunity to catch up and utter the immortal line, "Thanks for the ride, lady!" The zombie hitchhiker continues to pursue immoral Annie, and, terrified and angry, she basically "kills" the hitchhiker over and over by repeatedly hitting him with her car. But he just won't lie down, and he expresses nothing other than gratitude for her very kind lift. In the EC horror tradition, "The Hitchhiker" makes it difficult to feel bad for the inevitable death of such a morally bankrupt protagonist; the real tragedy here is the eventual demise of Annie's luxury Mercedes-Benz.

OPPOSITE: **Zombified hands burst through the surface of a road in this Johnny Craig cover for** *The Vault of Horror* **#26. The EC comic book series was the inspiration for the 1973 Amicus horror flick of the same name.**

TOP LEFT: **EC Comics artist Jack Kamen's poster for the 1982 George A. Romero-directed movie** *Creepshow* **plays on the style of classic EC titles like** *Tales from the Crypt* **and** *The Haunt of Fear.* **The film was written by horror maestro Stephen King.**

ABOVE: **The 1987 sequel to** *Creepshow* **again boasted an EC Comics homage poster. This time the movie was directed by Michael Gornick, George Romero's cinematographer on the original** *Creepshow.*

Zombie Comics in the Eighties and Nineties

The EC Comics horror revival may have started in film—unfettered as it was by the Comics Code Authority—but once the deaths of *Creepy* and *Eerie* had left a giant hole in the horror comics publishing market, publishers found new direct-to-market distribution channels that bypassed the CCA entirely, and new EC-esque titles began to spring up in their place.

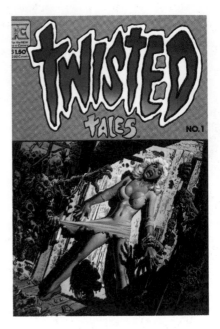

ABOVE: **Richard Corben's zombie-rific cover for the debut issue of Pacific Comics' *Twisted Tales*, November 1982.**

The first issue of *Twisted Tales* came out in late 1982 in the tried-and-true bimonthly anthology format. Unlike *Creepy* and *Eerie*, though, *Twisted* featured full-color interiors in the traditional comic—rather than magazine—style. It only lasted ten issues, but it certainly made a splash with its EC-inspired hyper-gore, gratuitous nudity, and twist endings, as well as the fact that it was illustrated by some of the best horror artists of the day, including Bernie Wrightson, John Bolton, Richard Corben, and Alfredo Alcala. Zombies once again figured often in the narratives; a story starring the classic EC revenge zombie, "Out of His Depth," appears in the very first issue. *Twisted Tales* provided a direct thematic and stylistic link to EC's legacy in the eighties, but it wouldn't be until later in the decade that zombies would become the stars of their own series.

Deadworld—written and created by Stuart Kerr and Ralph Griffith, and illustrated by then-newbie Vince Locke—was first released in 1987. Although the ownership of and creative force behind the comic has changed hands, and it has jumped publishers a few times, new issues are still being published through Image Comics, making it one of the longest-lasting (if not continuously published) zombie comics ever. In a complete reversal from the Romero blueprint, the zombies in *Deadworld* are the result of a supernatural plague and, while they are dead, they have fully realized personalities of their own (they even ride Harleys!). However, the narrative does focus on the human condition when faced with a zombie apocalypse, rather than on the machinations of the zombies themselves, a tactic that is a hallmark of the Romero film.

Deadworld was followed closely by more zombie-focused comics, such as *Deadwalkers* (beginning in 1991 from Aircel Comics), *King of the Dead* (1994, FantaCo Entertainment), and a monthly graphic adaptation of everyone's favorite silly, low-budget gorefest film *Army of Darkness* (1992, Dark Horse). The first three issues of the comic comprised a simple adaptation of the film, illustrated by John Bolton and written by Sam and Ivan Raimi. Later issues expanded on the original story and saw Ash battling not just the zombie-esque Deadites but also classic Universal monsters—Dracula, Frankenstein, the Wolfman—and the series featured crossovers with Lovecraft's Re-Animator, Freddy Krueger, and Jason Voorhees. Later, during the zombie comic explosion of the 2000s, Ash would be called to crossover with *Marvel Zombies*.

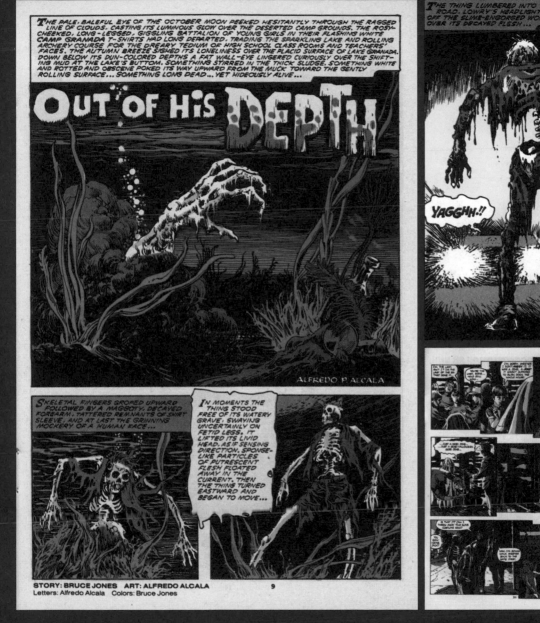

OUT OF HIS DEPTH

THE PALE, BALEFUL EYE OF THE OCTOBER MOON PEEKED HESITANTLY THROUGH THE RAGGED LINE OF CLOUDS, CASTING ITS LUMINOUS GLOW OVER THE DESERTED CAMP GROUNDS. THE ROSY-CHEEKED, LONG-LEGGED, GIGGLING BATTALION OF YOUNG GIRLS IN THEIR FLASHING WHITE CAMP GRANADA T-SHIRTS HAD LONG DEPARTED, TRADING THE SPARKLING LAKE AND ROLLING ARCHERY COURSE FOR THE DREARY TEDIUM OF HIGH SCHOOL CLASS ROOMS AND TEACHERS' FACES. THE AUTUMN BREEZE SIGHED ITS LONELINESS OVER THE PLACID SURFACE OF LAKE GRANADA. DOWN BELOW ITS DUN-COLORED DEPTHS A FAT WALL-EYE LINGERED CURIOUSLY OVER THE SHIFT-ING MUD AT THE LAKE'S BOTTOM, SOMETHING STIRRED IN THE THICK SLUDGE, SOMETHING WHITE AND ROTTED AND OBSCENE POKED ITS WAY UPWARD FROM THE MUCK TOWARD THE GENTLY ROLLING SURFACE... SOMETHING LONG DEAD... YET HIDEOUSLY ALIVE...

THE THING LUMBERED INTO THE NARROW ROAD. LOWRY'S HEADLIGHTS REFLECTING OFF THE SLIME-ENGORGED WORMS CRAWLING OVER ITS DECAYED FLESH...

YAGGHH.!!

SKELETAL FINGERS GROPED UPWARD FOLLOWED BY A MAGGOTY, DECAYED FOREARM, TATTERED REMNANTS OF SHIRT SLEEVE, AND AT LAST THE GRINNING MOCKERY OF A HUMAN FACE...

IN MOMENTS THE THING STOOD FREE OF ITS WATERY GRAVE, SWAYING UNCERTAINLY ON FETID LEGS. IT LIFTED ITS LIVID HEAD, AS IF SENSING DIRECTION, SPONGE-LIKE PARTICLES OF PUTRESCENT FLESH FLOATED AWAY IN THE CURRENT. THEN THE THING TURNED EASTWARD AND BEGAN TO MOVE...

ALFREDO P. ALCALA

STORY: BRUCE JONES   ART: ALFREDO ALCALA
Letters: Alfredo Alcala   Colors: Bruce Jones

9

ABOVE LEFT: **In the** *Twisted Tales* **story "Out of His Depth" by Bruce Jones and Alfred Alcala, a zombie rises from the depths of a lake to seek revenge on the woman who murdered him. Like many** *Twisted Tales* **stories, it owes a debt to the**

TOP: **Willie the dead janitor lurches into the headlamps of a car in "Out of His Depth" from** *Twisted Tales.*

ABOVE: **Bruce Jones and Tim Conrad's** *Twisted Tales* **story "All Hallows" features a zombified kid returning**

Zombie Comics in the New Millennium

While *Resident Evil* was staging a zombie revolution in video games in the late 1990s and *28 Days Later* performed a similar role in film in the early 2000s, zombies took a backseat to more general horror-themed comics such as *Hellblazer*, *Swamp Thing*, and, at times, *Sandman*. That is, until *The Walking Dead* put zombies back behind the wheel.

First published in 2003 through Image, Robert Kirkman's *The Walking Dead* begins with a similar premise to *28 Days Later*: a man, in this case a cop, is shot and falls into a coma. When he wakes up weeks later, the world has changed drastically—a zombie apocalypse, caused by an unspecified infection, has decimated the world, leaving only bands of survivors to face the hoards. Unlike *28 Days Later*, however, the zombies in *Walking Dead* are Romero archetypes—dead, slow, and completely mindless, driven only by some deep instinct for human flesh. Once again, the survivors and their character developments are the main attraction; the zombies serve only as a catalyst and source of conflict.

Considering the trends in other media at the turn of the millennium, it was only a matter of time before zombies became a talking point in comics again, but *The Walking Dead* is most cited as renewing serious interest in zombie-themed comics. The series is ongoing and shows no sign of ending any time soon; in the meantime, other creators and publishers have spotted the demand for undead comics, sparking a host of new titles. In 2004, George Romero created an original six-

The debut issue of Robert Kirkman's epic zombie comic *The Walking Dead*, October 2003, with cover art by original series artist Tony Moore.

From *The Walking Dead* #1, police officer Rick Grimes wakes up from a coma and encounters zombies for the first time. Art by Tony Moore.

Protected from the zombie hordes by barricades, the residents of a small town pass the time with gladiatorial contests—with added undead hazards—in *The Walking Dead* #28. Art by Charlie Adlard.

Having taken refuge in a prison, and beset on all sides by the living dead, the survivors of the zombie plague come to a startling revelation in *The Walking Dead* #24. Art by Charlie Adlard.

169

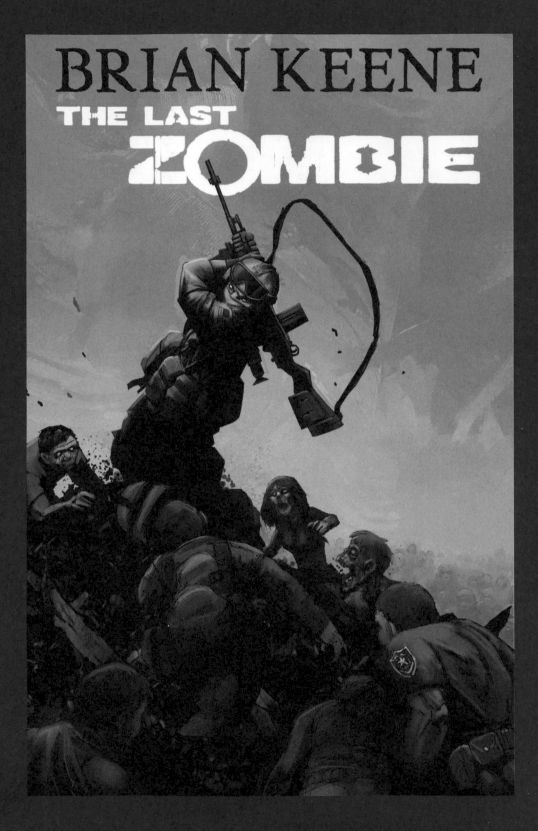

issue zombie comic titled *Toe Tags* and published through DC; at the same time, Steve Niles of *30 Days of Night* fame wrote a comic adaptation of *Dawn of the Dead* (the original, not the 2004 remake). In the same year, Niles also published a modern adaptation of Shelley's *Frankenstein* in comic form.

Marvel decided to get in on the undead action in 2005, when Robert Kirkman wrote the five-issue *Marvel Zombies* for their MAX Imprint, which portrays Marvel's most popular superheroes as ravenous flesh-eating zombies. In a departure from *The Walking Dead* and most zombie stories, *Marvel Zombies* focuses on the story of the zombies themselves; in this case, they're completely sentient and only turn into frenzied monsters when they haven't eaten human flesh for a while. The narrative follows the super-zombies' quest to find a new food source after they've depleted Earth's supply of humans. Having proved himself a comics' innovator with *Walking Dead*, Kirkman shows us a new way to think about zombies—as the stars, rather than just the outside source of conflict—opening up new possibilities for zombie comics and narratives in the new millennium. Which is a good thing, since the current trend of zombie tales continues to stay strong, and the AMC

television adaptation of *The Walking Dead* can only give the movement even more momentum.

In the past decade, zombies have become a mainstay of all creative media, creeping slowly but surely into books, film, television, video games, comics, and now, increasingly, online. As we've seen, they've been around since the beginning, of course, enjoying periods of popularity and times when they were less regarded. But now, as we find ourselves well entrenched in this new millennium with all the accompanying societal fears it brings—rapidly advancing technology, bio-warfare, cloning, terrorism, bird flu; the worst atrocities we can imagine and even those we can't—zombies have proved themselves to be a prevalent and universal staple of horror, one that neatly expresses our fears of the new and unknown while allowing us to have a little fun with them. They are the monster that just keeps coming back to life—the true undead of popular culture.

Picture credits

All images are copyright © their respective copyright holders and are shown here for historical and review purposes. Every effort has been made to credit the copyright holders, artists, and/or studios/publishers whose work has been reproduced in these pages. We apologise for any omissions, which will be corrected in future editions, but must hereby disclaim any liability.

2   *I Walked with a Zombie*
© 1943 RKO Radio Pictures

4   *Evil Dead II* © 1987 De Laurentiis Entertainment Group/Renaissance Pictures

6–7   All images courtesy Robert L. Lucas.
Night of the Living Dead © 1968 Image Ten

9   *The Plague of the Zombies*
© 1966 Hammer Film Productions
City of the Living Dead © 1980 Dania Film.
Image courtesy Jay Slater
The Cabinet of Dr. Caligari
© 1920 Decla-Bioscop AG

10   *Invasion of the Body Snatchers*
© 1956 Walter Wanger Productions
Shock Waves © 1977 Zopix Company.
Image courtesy Blue Underground

11   *Let Sleeping Corpses Lie* © 1974 Star Films S.A. Image courtesy Blue Underground

12   Alexander King illustration from Seabrook's *The Magic Island*, Literary Guild of America, 1929

14   Photo from Seabrook's *The Magic Island*, Literary Guild of America, 1929

15   Photo from Seabrook's *The Magic Island*, Literary Guild of America, 1929

16–17   Alexander King illustrations from Seabrook's *The Magic Island*, Literary Guild of America, 1929

18   Engraving from Voltaire's *Candide*, 1787

19   *Execrable Human Traffick, or The Affectionate Slaves*, George Morland, 1789

20   Alfred Rondier, *Frank Leslie's Illustrated Newspaper*, 1878 *Cannibal Cousins*, Minton, Balch & Company, 1934

21   *Black Bagdad*, A.L. Burt Company, 1933

22   Bokor image © Wade Davis
Photograph of Wade Davis

23   *White Zombie* © 1932 United Artists

24   *The Serpent and the Rainbow*
© 1988 Serpent and the Rainbow/
Universal Pictures

25   *The Serpent and the Rainbow*,
Pocket Books, 1997
Zombie powder image © Wade Davis

26   *White Zombie* © 1932 United Artists

28   Stories from the Arabian Nights,
Scribner's, 1907
Theodor von Holst, frontispiece from
Frankenstein, 1831

29   Harry Clarke, "The Premature Burial," *Tales of Mystery and Imagination*, Harrap, 1928
Harry Clarke, "Ligeia," *Tales of Mystery and Imagination*, Harrap, 1928
Harry Clarke, "The Facts in the Case of M. Valdemar," *Tales of Mystery and Imagination*, Harrap, 1919

30   E. M. Stevenson, *Weird Tales* September 1926, Popular Fiction Publishing Co.
Hennes Bok, *Weird Tales* March 1940, Popular Fiction Publishing Co.,
© coll. Maison s'Ailleurs/Agence Martienne

31   Artist unknown, *Strange Tales* June 1932, The Clayton Magazine, Inc.

32   Poster and still from *The Cabinet of Dr. Caligari*, 1920. *The Cabinet of Dr. Caligari* © 1920 Decla-Bioscop AG

33   Stills from *White Zombie*
© 1932 United Artists

34   *White Zombie* © 1932 United Artists

35   *The Mummy* © 1931 Universal Pictures

36   *The Walking Dead*
© 1936 Warner Bros. Pictures

37   *The Ghoul* © 1933 Gaumont British Picture Corporation

38   *The Man They Could Not Hang*
© 1939 Columbia Pictures Corporation

39   *The Revolt of the Zombies*
© 1936 Edward Halperin Productions
The Living Dead
© 1934 British International Pictures

40   *The Ghost Breakers*
© 1940 Paramount Pictures

41   *King of the Zombies*
© 1941 Monogram Pictures
Bowery at Midnight
© 1942 Banner Productions
Revenge of the Zombies
© 1943 Monogram Pictures

42   *The Mad Ghoul* © 1943 Universal Pictures

43   *Voodoo Man* © 1944 Banner Productions

44   *I Walked with a Zombie*
© 1943 RKO Radio Pictures

45   *Zombies on Broadway*
© 1945 RKO Radio Pictures

46   *Scared Stiff* © 1953 Paramount Pictures

47   *Creature with the Atom Brain*
© 1955 Clover Productions
Invasion of the Body Snatchers
© 1956 Walter Wanger Productions
Quatermass 2/Enemy from Space
© 1957 Hammer Film Productions

48   *Zombies of Mora Tau*
© 1957 Clover Productions
Voodoo Island
© 1957 Aubrey Schenck Productions
The Thing that Couldn't Die
© 1958 Universal International Pictures

49   *Invisible Invaders*
© 1959 Robert E. Kent Productions
Plan 9 from Outer Space
© 1959 Reynolds Pictures

50   *The Dead One*
© 1961 Mardi Gras Productions
The Incredibly Strange Creatures…
© 1964 Morgan-Steckler Productions

51   *Tales of Terror* © 1962 Alta Vista Productions

52   *I Eat Your Skin*
© 1964 Iselin-Tenney Productions
The Horror of Party Beach
© 1964 Iselin-Tenney Productions

53   *The Astro-Zombies* © 1968 Ram Ltd.

54   *Santo vs. the Zombies*
© 1962 Filmadora Panamericana
Doctor Blood's Coffin
© 1961 Caralan Productions

55   *The Earth Dies Screaming*
© 1965 Lippert Films
The Frozen Dead
© 1966 Gold Star/Seven Arts
Dr. Terror's House of Horrors
© 1965 Amicus Productions

56   *The Plague of the Zombies*
© 1966 Hammer Film Productions/
Seven Arts

57   *War of the Zombies* © 1964 Galatea Film
Bloody Pit of Horror © 1965 International Entertainment/M.B.S. Cinematografica
Terror Creatures from the Grave © 1965 G.I.A. Cinematografica/International Entertainment/M.B.S. Cinematografica
Planet of the Vampires © 1965 AIP/
Castilla Cooperativa Cinematográfica/
Italian International Film
The Last Man on Earth
© 1964 Produzioni La Regina/AIP

58   Image courtesy Blue Underground.
The Ghost Galleon
© 1974 Ancla Century Films/Belén Films

61–65   All images courtesy Robert L. Lucas.
Night of the Living Dead © 1968 Image Ten

66   *Tombs of the Blind Dead*
© 1971 Interfilme/Plata Films S.A.

67   Images courtesy Blue Underground.
Tombs of the Blind Dead
© 1971 Interfilme/Plata Films S.A.

68   *Return of the Blind Dead*
© 1973 Ancla Century Films.
Images courtesy Blue Underground.
The Ghost Galleon
© 1974 Ancla Century Films/Belén Films.
Image courtesy Blue Underground

69   *The Ghost Galleon*
© 1974 Ancla Century Films/Belén Films.
Image courtesy Blue Underground
Grapes of Death © 1978 Films A.B.C.

70   *Let Sleeping Corpses Lie*
© 1974 Star Films S.A./Flaminia
Produzioni Cinematografiche.
Top right image courtesy Blue Underground

71   *Tales from the Crypt*
© 1972 Amicus Productions

72   *Horror Express*
© 1972 Benmar Productions/Granada Films

73   *Deathdream*
© 1974 Impact Films/Quadrant Films

74   *Sugar Hill* © 1974 AIP

75   Images courtesy Blue Underground.
Shock Waves © 1977 Zopix Company

76–77   *Dawn of the Dead* © 1978 Laurel Group

78–79   *Zombie*
© 1978 Variety Film Productions

80   *Return of the Living Dead*
© 1978 Hemdale Films/Fox Films

82   *City of the Living Dead*
© 1980 Dania Film/Medusa Distribuzione/
National Cinematografica

83 *City of the Living Dead*
© 1980 Dania Film/Medusa Distribuzione/
National Cinematografica.
Bottom left image courtesy Jay Slater
The Beyond © 1981 Fulvia Film.
Bottom right image courtesy Jay Slater

84 *The House by the Cemetery*
© 1981 Fluvia Film
Zombie 3 © 1988 Flora Film.
Image courtesy Jay Slater

85 *Cannibal Apocalypse* © 1980 Edmondo
Amati presents/José Frade Producciones
Cinematográficas S.A./New Fida.
Image courtesy Jay Slater
Zombie Holocaust © 1980 Aquarius
Productions/Dania Film/Flora Film.
Image courtesy Jay Slater
Porno Holocaust © 1981 Kristal Film

86 *Hell of the Living Dead*
© 1980 Beatrice Film/Films Dara.
Image courtesy Jay Slater
Burial Ground © 1981 Esteban
Cinematografica. Image courtesy Jay Slater
The Devil Hunter © 1980 Eurociné/
J.E. Films/Lisa-Film.

87 *Zombie Lake* © 1981 Eurociné/J.E. Films.
Images courtesy Jay Slater
The Living Dead Girl © 1982 Films A.B.C.
Devil Story © 1985 Condor Films
Productions

88 *Friday the 13th* © 1980 Georgetown
Productions Inc./Paramount Pictures/
Sean S. Cunningham Films

89 *The Fog* © 1980 AVCO Embassy Pictures/EDI.
Image courtesy Michael Felsher
Prince of Darkness
© 1987 Universal Pictures/Alive Films

90 *Dead and Buried* © 1981 Barclays
Mercantile Industrial Finance
Creepshow © 1982 Creepshow Films Inc./
Laurel Entertainment Inc./Warner Bros.

91 *Thriller* © 1983 Optimum Productions.
Image courtesy Paul Davis
Creepshow © 1982 Creepshow Films Inc./
Laurel Entertainment Inc.

92–93 *Evil Dead II* © 1987 De Laurentiis
Entertainment Group/Renaissance Pictures;
right two images courtesy
Greg Nicotero

94 *Return of the Living Dead*
© 1978 Hemdale Films/Fox Films.
Bottom image courtesy Michael Felsher

95 Images courtesy Michael Felsher.
Re-Animator © 1985 Empire Pictures/
Re-Animator Productions

96–97 *Day of the Dead* © 1985 Dead Films Inc./
Laurel Entertainment Inc./Laurel-Day Inc.
Top left image p. 96 courtesy Michael Felsher

98 *Night of the Creeps* © 1986 TriStar
Pictures/Delphi V Productions.
Image courtesy Michael Felsher
Maniac Cop © 1988 Shapiro-Glickenhaus
Home Video
The Serpent and the Rainbow © 1988
Serpent and the Rainbow/Universal
Pictures. Image courtesy Michael Felsher

100 *Bride of Re-Animator* © 1990 Wild Street.
Images courtesy Michael Felsher

101 *Return of the Living Dead III* © 1993 Bandai
Visual Company/Ozla Productions

102–103 *Night of the Living Dead* © 1990 21st
Century Film Corporation/Columbia
Pictures Corporation

104 *Two Evil Eyes*
© 1990 ADC Films/Gruppo Bema
Braindead © 1992 WingNut Films
Death Becomes Her
© 1992 Universal Pictures

105 *Cemetery Man* © 1994 Audiofilm/
Bibo Productions/Canal+

106 *Dead Snow* © 2009 Euforia Film/
Barentsfilm AS/Miho Film

108 *Biohazard* © Capcom

109 *Wild Zero* © 2000 Dragon Pictures/GAGA/
Takeuchi Entertainment. Poster courtesy
Colin Geddes

110 *The Happiness of the Katakuris* © 2001
Katakuri-ke no Kôfuku Seisaku Iinkai/
Shochiku Company. Top right image
courtesy Tom Mes at midnighteye.com

111 *Battlefield Baseball* © 2003 Klock Worx Co./
Media Suits/napalm FiLMS
Tokyo Zombie © 2005 Tôkyô Zonbi
Seisaku Iinkai

112 *Resident Evil* © 2002 Sony Pictures

113 *Resident Evil: Apocalypse*
© 2004 Sony Pictures

114 *Resident Evil* © 2002 Sony Pictures

115 *Doom* © 2005 Universal
The Dead Hate the Living
© 2000 Full Moon Entertainment

116 *28 Days Later* © 2002 Fox Searchlight

117 *28 Weeks Later* © 2007 20th Century Fox

118 *Undead* © 2003 Spierigfilm

119 *Shaun of the Dead* © 2004 Universal Pictures

120 *Dawn of the Dead*
© 2004 Strike Entertainment/Universal

121 *Dawn of the Dead*
© 2004 Strike Entertainment/Universal

122 *Masters of Horror* © 2005/2006 IDT
Entertainment/Starz Productions.
Images Courtesy Anchor Bay Entertainment

123 *Land of the Dead* © 2005 Universal Pictures

124 *Fido* © 2005 Lions Fate Films
Slither © 2006 Strike Entertainment/
Universal
Mulberry Street © 2006 Belladonna
Productions/Mulberry Street Films LLC

125 *Re-Penetrator* © 2004 and courtesy
BurningAngel.com
Zombie Strippers © 2008 Sony Pictures

126 *Planet Terror* © 2007 Dimension Films
Doghouse © 2009 Carnaby International

127 *Dead Snow* © 2009 Euforia Film/
Barentsfilm AS/Miho Film
Zibahkhana
© 2007 Bubonic Films/Mondo Macabro
Zombieland © 2009 Columbia Pictures
Pontypool © 2008 Ponty Up Pictures/
Shadow Shows

128 *Diary of the Dead* © 2007 Artfire Films/
Romero-Grunwald Productions
Survival of the Dead © 2009 Blank of the
Dead Productions/Devonshire Productions/
New Romero

129 *[Rec]* © 2007 Filmax
[Rec 2] © 2009 Filmax
The 4th Reich © 2010 Nomarite
Productions/Philm Distribution/
Smudge Film Productions

130 *Dead Rising 2* © 2010 Capcom
132 *Book of the Dead*: Bantam
133 *The Mammoth Book of Zombies*: Robinson
134 *Steven the Zombie*: Bantam
Zombie Survival Guide/*Recorded Attacks*:
Three Rivers Press
135 *World War Z*: Three Rivers Press
The Rising/*City of the Dead*: Leisure Books/
Dorchester Publishing
136–137 *Monster Island*/*Monster Nation*/*Monster
Planet*: Snowbooks
138 *Cell*: Scribner
The Stupidest Angel: Orbit
139 *Pride and Prejudice and Zombies*:
Quirk Books
Pride and Prejudice and Zombies GN:
Titan Books
141 *Cell*: Hodder & Stoughton
One Rainy Night: Headline
142 *The Evil Dead* game © Palace Software
Zombie Zombie © Quicksilva
143 *Monkey Island 2: LeChuck's Revenge*
© LucasArts
Corpse Killer © Digital Pictures
144–145 *Resident Evil/Survivor/Zero/Resident Evil 4/
Resident Evil 5* all © Capcom
146 *House of the Dead*/*Overkill* © Sega
Evil Dead: Regeneration © THQ
147 *Dead Rising* © Capcom
148–149 *Left 4 Dead*/*Left 4 Dead 2*
© Valve Corporation
150 *Walk Among Us*: Rhino/WEA; © Misfits
Famous Monsters: Roadrunner; © Misfits
151 *Thriller* © 1983 Optimum Productions.
Image courtesy Paul Davis
152 *Astro-Creep: 2000*: Geffen; © White Zombie
Hellbilly Deluxe: Geffen; © Rob Zombie
153 All images © and courtesy Zombeatles
154 Photo © Dash Revery
155 Top two photos © Dash Revery;
lower photo © Laura Willis
156–158 *Masters of Horror* © 2005/2006 IDT
Entertainment/Starz Productions
159 Images courtesy Sipa Press/Rex Features
160–161 All images © Gaines Estate
162–163 All images © 2010 New Comic Company
164 *The Vault of Horror* © Gaines Estate
165 *Creepshow* © 1982 Creepshow Films Inc./
Laurel Entertainment Inc./Warner Bros.
Creepshow 2 © 1987 Laurel Entertainment
Inc./New World Pictures
166 *Twisted Tales* © 1982 Pacific Comics
167 "Out of his Depth" © 1982 Bruce Jones/
Alfred Alcala
"All Hallows" © 1982 Bruce Jones/
Tim Conrad
168–169 *The Walking Dead* © 2011 Robert Kirkman
170 *The Last Zombie* © 2010 Brian Keene
171 *Marvel Zombies* © 2006 Marvel Comics
Blackgas © 2006 Warren Ellis
Crossed © 2008 Garth Ennis

173

Index

"The grave's a fine and private place, but none, I think, do there embrace."

Andrew Marvell

Jovanka Vuckovic would like to thank the following people, without whom this book would not have been possible: Augustine Books, Donna Davies, George Romero, Clark Savage, Jr. of The Nostalgia League, Frédéric Jaccaud, Terry Nudds, Neil Mechem of Girasol Collectables, Dr. Macro's High Quality Movie Scans, William Forsche, Bill Lustig and Greg Chick at Blue Undergound, Robert Lucas, Thea Munster, Jay Slater, Micheal R. Felsher of Red Shirt Pictures, Anchor Bay Entertainment, Amy at Dark Horse Comics, Tom Mes, Colin Geddes, Mick Garris, Ed Peters, Anchor Bay Entertainment, Edgar Wright, Steve Niles and Peter and Michael Spierig.

For Shane and Violet Faulkner, who brought me back to life.